THOMAS JEFFERSON

PART I
Introduction 3

PART II
BORN TO PRIVILEGE
Early Education 7
Inheritance and More Learning 10
Lawyer and Politician 12

PART III
MARRIAGE AND MONTICELLO
Marriage, Family, and Sorrow 17
Return to Politics 20

PART IV
REVOLUTION AND NATION BUILDING
Declaration of Independence 25
The State of Virginia 28
Congress and Foreign Affairs 31
Secretary of State 34
Election of 1796 37

PART V
PRESIDENCY
Chief Executive 41
First Barbary War 43
Louisiana Purchase 48
Expeditions 50
Native American Policies 52

PART VI
SECOND TERM

Challenges   57
Aaron Burr   60
The Chesapeake-Leopard Affair   63

PART VII
RETURN TO PRIVATE LIFE
University of Virginia   69
Jefferson and Adams   71
Autobiography   73
Lafayette   75
Sunset   77

PART VIII
LEGACY
Government   81
Religion   83
Banks   85
Slavery   87
The Sally Hemings Question   90

PART IX
The Measure of a Man   93

PART X
Bibliography   95

ALEXANDER HAMILTON

PART I
The Orphan of the Caribbean   99

PART II
The New Boy in New York   105

PART III
A Revolutionary for Washington   111

PART IV
A Commanding Critic and a Man of the
Constitution   119

PART V
A Titan of the Treasury: Reports   125

THOMAS JEFFERSON & ALEXANDER HAMILTON

Two Lifelong Rivals

THE HISTORY HOUR

HISTORY

PART VI
A Titan of the Treasury II: The Two-Party Tango   135

PART VII
Resignation, the Reynolds Affair, and Wounds   143

PART VIII
A Flawed Man Through and Through   153

PART IX
Further reading   157

Your Free eBook!   159

THOMAS JEFFERSON

Patriot. Statesman. President

❧ I ❧
INTRODUCTION

"One man with courage is a majority."

— THOMAS JEFFERSON

❦

Founding father. Patriot. Statesman. President.

❦

Thomas Jefferson was all of these things and more. He was one of the men who helped to bring the United States into being, and he shepherded the country through some of the most dynamic political years in its history. It is very possible that without his brilliance, the fledgling democracy, the first in the world since the end of Ancient Greece, may not have survived its first few trials by fire.

꠵

Jefferson was a great man. He was also a complicated man and a man whose moral convictions were unwavering in some areas and completely conflicted in others.

꠵

To many of us, he is like a statue, a perfect image of a man frozen in marble. Look more closely, though, and you can see that the statue has feet of clay.

❧ II ❧
BORN TO PRIVILEGE

"I like the dreams of the future better than the history of the past."

— THOMAS JEFFERSON

❧

Thomas Jefferson was born on April 13, 1743, as a subject of the British Crown. He was the third of ten children of Peter Jefferson and Jane Randolph, who at the time of his birth lived at Shadwell in the Colony of Virginia, in the shadow of the Blue Ridge Mountains. He was part of the well-to-do elite. Peter Jefferson was a planter and surveyor in the County of Albemarle. His mother was the daughter of Isham Randolph, a sea captain who was the son of William Randolph, one of the wealthiest planters in all of Virginia.

Theirs was a large family, as was normal at the time: Jane, who would die a spinster; Mary, who would marry a member of the Virginia House of Burgesses; Thomas Jefferson himself; Elizabeth; Martha, who would marry Jefferson's best friend, Dabney Carr; two boys named Peter, both of whom died in infancy; Lucy; and lastly the twins, Anna and Randolph.

EARLY EDUCATION

❦

I n 1745, Colonel William Randolph, Jane Randolph Jefferson's grandfather, and Peter Jefferson's close friend passed away, leaving Peter as the executor of his estate and the guardian of his infant son, Jefferson Mann Randolph. The estate that Randolph left behind was a plantation called Tuckahoe. In order to attend to his new duties, Peter relocated the family from Shadwell to Tuckahoe. Thomas Jefferson later recorded that his first memory arose from this time when he recalled being carried on a pillow by a slave during the family's move. Slavery would shadow Jefferson until the end of his life.

❦

While he was at Tuckahoe, Jefferson began his education with private tutors. His father regretted never having had a proper education of his own, so he pushed young Jefferson, his first-born son, to enter school early. He began his studies at the tender age of five years old.

❧

The family returned to Shadwell in 1752, when Jefferson was nine years old. He was enrolled in a local school run by a Presbyterian minister from Scotland. His learning incorporated Latin, Greek and French, and he began to study the natural world, which would remain a lifelong passion. He also learned horseback riding and spent many hours reading the books in his father's library.

❧

In 1758, his tutelage passed to Reverend James Maury, who ran a boarding school near Gordonsville, Virginia. It was not a boarding school in the traditional sense; rather, Reverend Maury hosted the children that he taught, and they lived in his home with his family. Here, he added history, science, music and the classics (Cicero, Homer, Plato, and Aristotle among them) to his curriculum. He traveled to Williamsburg with Reverend Maury and met Patrick Henry, the future patriot, who was eight years old than Jefferson but whom he came to like a great deal unless they were arguing against one another in court. The two bonded over their common love of music, specifically the violin, which they both played. He stayed with Maury for two years, returning to Shadwell in 1760.

❧

At that time, Virginia was on the frontier, and Jefferson came to know many Native American traders who stopped over at

Shadwell while they were traveling to Williamsburg for business. Among these Native Americans was the Cherokee chief Ontassete. When Chief Ontassete took his leave of his people before he made the perilous trip to London, Jefferson was in attendance. The chief's oratory and the connection he had with his people moved him, and he vowed that he would try to emulate the chief's eloquent example.

INHERITANCE AND MORE LEARNING

❧

When Jefferson was only 14 years old, his father died, leaving his estate to be divided between Jefferson and his brother, Randolph. Jefferson's share of the inheritance was about 5,000 acres of land and between 20 and 40 slaves. He was able to take full command of the property once he turned 21. Despite the beauty of the place and lucrative nature of the inheritance, he dreamed of living on a mountain.

❧

When he was 16 years old, only two years after his father's death, Jefferson entered the College of William and Mary in Williamsburg. His professor, William Small, taught him mathematics, metaphysics, and philosophy, and he introduced him to some of the premier minds of his day. These included George Wythe, a brilliant law professor, and Francis Fauquier, the Lieutenant Governor of Virginia Colony. Fauquier used to throw lavish parties, and Jefferson was invited to them all, where he would play the violin, flirt with ladies and drink expensive, imported wine. More serious companions were British Empiricists and philosophers like John Locke, Francis Bacon, and Isaac Newton, all of whom had a strong influence on Jefferson. He was befriended and invited into their inner circle, and on Friday nights he and these learned men would gather to discuss politics and philosophical questions of the day.

⟊⟨⟩⟊

Although he was much impressed by geniuses around him, he was still a young man, and he wasted much time and money in his first year at the college on the parties that Fauquier would throw. He quickly regretted his profligacy and dedicated himself to rigorous study at the beginning of his second year. He would study for fourteen hours every day, and his skills at French, Greek, and the violin improved immensely. He graduated in 1762 after only two years.

⟊⟨⟩⟊

He took work as a law clerk in the office of Professor Wythe, who taught him the law and helped him to obtain his law license. Jefferson was always a voracious reader, and he read English classics, political treatises, law, philosophy, history, natural law, *"natural religion,"* ethics, architecture, botany, and agriculture. Professor Wythe was so impressed by his intellect and driven curiosity that when he died, he bequeathed his entire library to Jefferson. His love of reading was a quality he never lost, and in later years, he stated,

"I cannot live without books."

LAWYER AND POLITICIAN

❧❧❧

J efferson became a licensed attorney in 1767 after he passed the Virginia bar. He also began his political career, representing the county of Albemarle in the Virginia House of Burgesses, one of the houses of civilian government in the colony. He served from 1769 until 1775.

❧❧❧

Among Jefferson's efforts in the House of Burgesses were a series of attempts to reform slavery. In the colonies, the Governor of Virginia and the Royal Court had the last word on the emancipation of slaves. In 1769, he introduced legislation to change that. He wanted masters to have the right to emancipate their slaves as they wished, and even persuaded his cousin, Richard Bland, to join him in attempting to pass the bill. The Burgesses' reaction was strongly negative, and the law was never passed.

He turned instead to his legal practice, where he accepted several cases for slaves seeking freedom, which he took on pro bono, meaning he waived his fee. While arguing for the freedom of one client, who sought emancipation while he was still technically too young by law, Jefferson made his first argument in support of individual rights and personal liberty, which he stated were granted by God as part of Natural Law. The judge in the case refused to let him finish his statement and summarily ruled against his client. In response, Jefferson gave his enslaved client a large sum of money, and the client mysteriously vanished, heading north with Jefferson's assistance.

He had several notable cases that he argued before the highest court in the colony: *Howell v Netherland* (1770), in which he stated that all human beings are born free; *Bolling v Bolling* (1771), during which he and his old law professor Wythe argued for opposite sides; and *Blair v Blair* (1772), a scandalous divorce case that had such flagrantly sexual content that Jefferson's notes called the evidence *"**voluminous and indecent.**"* Legal scholars have called the Blair case the baby steps of the ideas of liberty that led to American independence.

❧ III ❧
MARRIAGE AND MONTICELLO

"The happiest moments of my life have been the few which I have passed at home in the bosom of my family."

— THOMAS JEFFERSON

❧

Jefferson had long wished to live on a mountain, and in his boyhood, he had spent many happy days playing on the 868-foot mountain that stood above his home in Shadwell. He named the mountain Monticello. In 1768, Jefferson hired workers and deployed his slaves to clear a 250 square foot patch of ground on the highest point of that mountain, and for the next forty years, he would design, build, tear down, and rebuild the house until it became the architectural showpiece that still stands today.

The first structure of Monticello was a small, single-room brick house with a walk-out basement and workshop. This came to be known as the South Pavilion, and in 1770, he took up residence in the house, which he had designed from the ground up, and which overlooked his 5,000-acre plantation.

MARRIAGE, FAMILY, AND
SORROW

☙⚬❧

On January 1, 1772, Thomas Jefferson married Martha Wayles Skelton, his 23-year-old widowed third cousin. She was a gifted household manager, a glittering hostess and blessed with both intellect and musical skill. She was an accomplished pianist, and Jefferson would often accompany her on violin or cello. She was also renowned for the delicacy and skill of her needlework. The years of their marriage were the happiest of Thomas's life, and together they had six children, only two of whom lived to adulthood: Martha, called Patsy; Jane, who lived only one year; a son who died nameless after two weeks; Mary Wayles, called Polly; Lucy Elizabeth, who died after one year; and another daughter named Lucy Elizabeth, who only lived for three years. Patsy and Polly were the only survivors, and though this was tragic, it was not terribly unusual for the time.

☙⚬❧

Martha's father died in 1773, and the couple inherited 135 slaves, including Martha's half-sister Sally Hemings. Under the law, any child born to an enslaved mother was herself automatically enslaved, and though Sally was as cultured, intelligent and educated as Martha, she remained a slave until her death. Future years would see Sally and Thomas Jefferson extremely close, and the controversy around their relationship survives to this day.

In addition to humans in bondage, Martha and Thomas also inherited an estate, a slave-trading business, and a mountain of debt. It took Jefferson years of effort to settle his late father-in-law's business liabilities, but he paid off everyone.

Martha was not a strong woman, nor a healthy one; her mother had died quite young, and she had endured difficult relationships with two stepmothers. During the ten years of their marriage, Martha bore many children, and with each pregnancy, her health declined. She died on September 6, 1782, only a few months after the birth of the last Lucy Elizabeth, with Jefferson at her bedside. Before her death, she made him swear to never remarry because she didn't want her daughters to suffer at the hands of a stepmother as she had done. He swore the oath as she requested.

Jefferson was nearly undone by his wife's death. He would spend long, grief-stricken nights pacing and weeping until he nearly dropped from exhaustion. He would take long, aimless rides with Patsy, and though he tried to conceal his suffering from his children, he would sometimes suffer "*violent bursts of grief.*" Some who knew him said that he never stopped grieving for his "*cherished companion.*"

RETURN TO POLITICS

෯෯

On December 16, 1773, a group of radical separatists calling themselves the Sons of Liberty boarded a ship in Boston Harbor that belonged to the British East India Tea Company. They were acting in opposition to the Townsend Acts, a set of laws passed by Parliament to undercut Colonial businesses in favor of companies based in Britain. Dressed as Native Americans, they tossed crates of tea overboard, destroying the entire valuable cargo. In retaliation, Parliament passed what came to be called the Intolerable Acts in 1774.

෯෯

Until these acts had passed, Massachusetts Colony had enjoyed a marked degree of autonomy and self-governance. These rights were granted by the Massachusetts Charter, which was revoked by the Intolerable Acts. The Acts also closed Boston Harbor to shipping until the Colonists paid reparations for the ruined tea shipment, effectively denying Boston merchants the right to trade. The acts were meant to punish Massachusetts for the actions of the Sons of Liberty, with the intention of forcing the wayward colony back into line. In response to these punitive measures, the colonists formed the First Continental Congress, and a body made up of representatives from all thirteen colonies which met in Philadelphia to determine their future course of action.

Jefferson wrote a resolution calling for a day of fasting and prayer and arguing that the people have the right to govern themselves. He also called for a boycott of all goods from Britain. He published his resolution under the title *A Summary View of the Rights of British America*. This treatise was presented to *the First Continental Congress* as a list of grievances against King George III and his government.

The Continental Congress forwarded their grievances to the king as a petition for change. The petition was ignored. The *Summary* was printed in pamphlet form and distributed widely in London, New York, and Philadelphia, which earned him a reputation as a skillful, persuasive and radical political thinker.

❦ IV ❦
REVOLUTION AND NATION BUILDING

"We hold these truths to be self-evident: that all men are created equal; that they are endowed by their Creator with certain unalienable rights; that among these are life, liberty and the pursuit of happiness."

— THOMAS JEFFERSON

❦

The lack of an acceptable response to their petition drove the colonists to convene a Second Continental Congress in 1775. This time, instead of trying to find a way to reconcile with their royal master in London, the colonists turned their attention to independence. They issued the Lee Resolution, which declared that the United Colonies were independent from Britain. The formal political revolution had begun.

DECLARATION OF
INDEPENDENCE

❦

In July 1776, the Colonies had been at war with Great Britain for almost a year, with the first battles being fought at Lexington and Concord in 1775. Despite the open hostilities, many colonists were still hoping that there might be some form of reconciliation with the Crown. When Parliament passed the Prohibitory Act in February 1776, which blockaded American ports and declared all American ships to be enemy vessels, the Massachusetts pro-independence firebrand John Adams stated that Parliament had already declared American independence and that it was time for the British Empire to be dismantled.

❦

Many Americans agreed. There were fully ninety different declarations of independence that circulated throughout the colonies, but there were none that every colony endorsed. The colonies were declaring themselves independent in a piecemeal fashion, but there needed to be a more uniform document to which all of the colonies agreed.

❧

Jefferson, one of the youngest delegates to the Second Continental Congress at 33 years old, was included in the Committee of Five, which was formed to draft a declaration of independence. Another member of the Committee of Five was John Adams, who would become one of Jefferson's closest friends and bitterest political rivals.

❧

The Committee of Five worked on the draft of the Declaration for seventeen days, with Jefferson doing most of the writing. He believed that Adams should be the principal author of the Declaration, but Adams pushed tor Jefferson to take the lead. He drew from a proposed draft of the Virginia Constitution that he had written as well as from the Virginia Declaration of Rights by George Mason. The other committee members made a few changes, and the finished draft was provided on June 28, 1776.

❧

Congress tinkered with the Declaration for two long days, arguing vehemently about what should and should not be included. There was a long passage that was deeply critical of the slave trade, claiming that Britain had forced the institution onto the colonies. The delegates from the southern colonies were all planters and slave owners, and after two days of debate, the passage was struck from the final document. The slavery passage was omitted so that the document would appear less radical, thereby not offending some individuals in the British Parliament who were secretly supportive of American independence. Jefferson never spoke publicly about the revisions, but he personally resented the changes that were imposed upon his document. He wrote privately that Congress had "*mangled*" his draft.

ॐ

The Congress ratified the Declaration of Independence on July 4, 1776, and all of the delegates signed it on August 2, 1776. There is a legend, possibly apocryphal, that when John Hancock placed his famously large-sized signature on the document, he said, urging unity of action,

"Now we must all hang together."

Benjamin Franklin supposedly responded,

"Yes, we must indeed all hang together, or most assuredly we shall all hang separately."

The act of signing the document was an act of treason against King George, and they all knew that if the revolution failed, their lives would be forfeit. Jefferson and his fellows showed great bravery in openly defying their imperial master.

THE STATE OF VIRGINIA

❧

When the revolution began, Jefferson held the rank of Colonel and was appointed the commander of the Albemarle County Militia. Almost immediately, in September 1776, he was elected to the Virginia House of Delegates to represent his county. For three years, he concentrated on writing the constitution for the State of Virginia. He entered legislation called the Bill for Establishing Religious Freedom, which prohibited state support or enforcement of religious institutions or beliefs. He also entered a bill seeking to disestablish the Anglican Church in Virginia. Both bills failed to pass.

❧

As one of the pre-eminent legal minds in the state, Jefferson was tasked with revising the entire corpus of Virginia's laws. He wrote 126 bills in three years, a monumental achievement and effort. His laws reformed the judicial system established requirements for standardized general education and attacked the "*feudal*" system of primogeniture which had dominated inheritance laws.

❧

Jefferson was elected as Governor of Virginia in 1779 and 1780, serving two one-year terms. During his tenure, he transferred the state capital from Williamsburg to Richmond and continued his work to reform and promote education, freedom of religion and revised inheritance laws.

❧

He was in Richmond when British forces marched on the city under the command of traitor Benedict Arnold, and he narrowly escaped with his life when the enemy burned the city to the ground. He was the target of a cavalry detachment sent by British General Charles Cornwallis, and he and other members of the Virginia General Assembly would have been captured had it not been for the intervention of Jack Jouett and the Virginia Militia. He took refuge his second plantation, Poplar Forest. There were suggestions that he had acted with cowardice, but an inquest by the Assembly determined that he had acted with honor.

❧

Jefferson received a letter from French diplomat François Barbé-Marbois in 1780, asking about the geography, history, and government of Virginia. He published his response in a book called *Notes on the State of Virginia*. Over the course of five years, he wrote an exhaustive study of his state, including reviews of scientific knowledge, history, politics, state law, natural resources, economy, culture, and geography. He also commented at length on slavery and miscegenation (mixing of the races). He believed that blacks and whites would never be able to coexist as free people because of the depth of resentment that would necessarily and rightly be caused by the institution of slavery.

❧

The book was first published in French in 1785, and an English language version was published in 1787. It was hailed as a great achievement and is still much respected, believed by many to be the most important American book published before 1800.

CONGRESS AND FOREIGN
AFFAIRS

❧

A fter the capitulation of the British army and the peace treaty that followed, the newborn United States formed a Congress of the Confederation. Jefferson was the delegate from Virginia. He joined a committee dedicated to setting foreign exchange rates, and it was his suggestion that American currency be based on the decimal system.

❧

Jefferson was chairman of a committee that was dedicated to establishing a new system of government for the nation, as well as to determine a standard set of rules for the settlement of western territories. The committee met during the 1783-1784 session of Congress. Jefferson proposed that Virginia should cede to the national government all of the territory it had claimed in the Ohio River basin, with the condition that the territory should be sectioned into areas that could in time become new states. He also suggested that slavery should be banned in all of the nation's territories. This bill was called the Land Ordinance of 1784, and it underwent a great deal of revision by Congress, including the elimination of the anti-slavery provision. This provision, called the "*Jefferson Proviso,*" was incorporated into the Northwest Ordinance of 1787.

భస

The Congress of the Confederation sent Jefferson to join Benjamin Franklin and John Adams in Europe, where he would work to negotiate trade agreements with England, Spain, and France. He spent five years in Paris as Minister to France, and his work there helped to shape the United States' foreign policy. He traveled to France with his daughter Patsy and two servants, including James Hemings, a slave and the older brother of Sally Hemings. He had James trained in the ways of French cooking, and he sent Patsy to be educated at the Pentemont Abbey.

భస

In 1786, he had a torrid six-week affair with Maria Cosway, an English/Italian musician. They were together frequently, but Maria had a husband. The affair ended when she returned to England, but the two continued to correspond for the rest of their lives.

భస

Jefferson sent for his daughter Patsy in June 1787, and she was accompanied by Sally Hemings, who was at that time 16 years old. While in Paris, it is believed that Jefferson and Sally began a sexual relationship, during which she became pregnant. According to an account written later by Sally's son Madison, she agreed to return to the United States on the condition that Jefferson would free her children when they reached the age of majority.

੭ॐਤੇ

During his stay in France, Jefferson became close friends with the Marquis de Lafayette, who had come to the aid of the colonies during the American revolution. The Marquis helped Jefferson to obtain trade agreements with the French crown. Jefferson was a supporter of the French Revolution, although he was uncomfortable with the more violent aspects of the undertaking. He was in Paris when revolutionaries stormed the Bastille, and he allowed the Marquis de Lafayette and his republican allies to meet at his residence. When the Marquis was writing the *Declaration of the Rights of Man and the Citizen*, Jefferson consulted with him and helped him draft the document.

SECRETARY OF STATE

❧

Jefferson returned to the United States in 1789 and accepted President George Washington's invitation to serve as Secretary of State. At that time, the two items of greatest concern were the national debt and the location of the capital.

❧

Jefferson believed that each state should be responsible for its debt, which put him in direct conflict with Alexander Hamilton, Secretary of the Treasury, who favored the consolidation of the states' debts into one debt held by the federal government. Hamilton was also dedicated to the establishment of a national bank, which Jefferson also opposed. He did everything he could to undermine Hamilton's plans, which so angered Washington that he nearly dismissed Jefferson from the cabinet.

❧✦❧

Jefferson and Hamilton sparred over the location of the capital, as well. Hamilton wanted to situate the capital in the Northeast, near the cities that formed the center of commerce in the fledgling nation. Jefferson, Washington and other members of the planter elite wanted the capital further to the south. The Compromise of 1790 settled the argument, with the capital being located on the banks of the Potomac River and the national government taking on the war debts of all of the states.

❧✦❧

In May 1792, Jefferson took umbrage at the developing political rivalries that he saw forming, and he wrote to Washington asking him to run for re-election, hoping that the great man would be a stabilizing influence. He wanted to create a political party to counter the Federalists, who were led by Alexander Hamilton. Jefferson espoused a position that would become the platform of the Democratic-Republican Party, which sought to increase states' rights and to oppose the sort of centralization of power that the Federalists pursued.

❧✦❧

While he was a member of Washington's cabinet, he was an enthusiastic supporter of France. When France and Britain entered into conflict in 1793, he pushed for the United States to support France against her enemy. His efforts were undermined by the antipathy that the French Revolutionary ambassador, Edmond-Charles Genêt, showed to President Washington.

❧

The interpersonal and political in-fighting caused Jefferson to develop migraines and garnered resentment from Washington. In December 1793, Jefferson resigned his cabinet position. Washington never forgave him, and the two men never spoke again. The animosity between the two was so great that when Washington died in 1799, Jefferson chose to remain at Monticello rather than attending his funeral.

❧

In 1794, Washington negotiated the Jay Treaty with Great Britain. The treaty was largely authored by Alexander Hamilton and formed an agreement whereby Britain relinquished territories in the Northwest that it had claimed in violation of the post-revolution peace treaty (the Treaty of Paris) in return for increased trade between the two countries. Jefferson saw this treaty as a serious overreach on the part of Jay and Hamilton, and he warned that it would undermine the republic and unduly increase Britain's influence. From Monticello, he organized a national resistance to the treaty, which became the Democratic-Republican Party.

ELECTION OF 1796

※

Jefferson ran for president in 1796 on the Democratic-Republican ticket, running against John Adams of the Federalist Party. He lost in the electoral college, but because of a quirk in the proceedings, he won the position of Vice President. He became the presiding officer of the Senate, but he limited his participation to issues of procedure, allowing the Senators to debate as they wished.

※

While he was Vice President, during the spring of 1797, Jefferson met four times with French consul Joseph Létombe. He attacked and undermined Adams and encouraged France to invade England. He also advised Létombe to stall any and all envoys to Paris sent by the Adams administration, which resulted in an openly hostile approach to the sitting president. Adams sent peace envoys to Paris, but they were rebuffed, an embarrassment that led Jefferson and his fellows

37

to call for a release of all documents related to the issue. Unfortunately, this backfired, as the documents revealed that French officials had demanded bribes. The incident, called the XYZ Affair, turned public opinion against France and led to an undeclared war between the two countries called the Quasi-War.

❧

The Adams administration passed the Alien and Sedition Acts, which Jefferson believed were both unconstitutional and aimed at suppressing his party. With the assistance of James Madison, he anonymously wrote the Kentucky and Virginia Resolutions. These resolutions permitted states to protect their citizens from federal laws that they believed were unconstitutional, something called interposition. Jefferson also advocated nullification, which was the right of states to invalidate objectionable federal laws completely. Washington was horrified by these resolutions, correctly recognizing in them the seed of future disunion. Nullification and interposition contributed to the American Civil War.

❧

Jefferson and Madison moved to Philadelphia in 1791 and founded the *National Gazette*, which was meant to directly counter the Federalist newspaper the *Gazette of the United States*, which had been created by Jefferson's old adversary, Alexander Hamilton. The *National Gazette* ran pieces by "Brutus" (James Madison) that sharply criticized Hamilton's policies and ideas. It was a war of words.

❧ V ❧

PRESIDENCY

"Politics is such a torment that I advise everyone I love not to mix with it."

— THOMAS JEFFERSON

❧❧❧

The 1800 Presidential election was one of the most heated and hateful affairs in all of American history. Jefferson ran once again at the head of the Democratic-Republican ticket, opposed by John Adams, who was seeking re-election. The incumbent was weakened by unpopular taxes and political backlash over the Quasi-War with France. Jefferson accused the Federalists of being secret monarchists; Adams accused Jefferson of being a libertine who was under the control of the French.

Ultimately, the Democratic-Republicans won more electoral college votes, but Jefferson and his running mate Aaron Burr received exactly the same number of votes in total. The election was decided by the House of Representatives, which was dominated by the Federalists. Alexander Hamilton unexpectedly argued in favor of a Jefferson win, relegating Burr to the office of vice president. Jefferson won the election.

When Adams had come to power, his administration had included many of the same people who had served under Washington, since Washington's people and Adams were all Federalists. Jefferson's administration would be drawn from his Democratic-Republican party faithful, with an almost wholesale reseating of the officers of government. This was accomplished with no violence and no strife. The election of 1800 was the first peaceful transition from one political party to another in American history.

CHIEF EXECUTIVE

❧

J efferson was sworn in on March 4, 1801, by Supreme Court Chief Justice John Marshall. Unlike his predecessors, Jefferson had no taste for formality or pomp. He rode to the inauguration on horseback, taking his horse to the stable himself. He was dressed plainly and came without any escort. His inaugural address stressed reconciliation with the Federalists, and his cabinet was made up of moderates. He was a fiercely political animal, but he came to Washington willing to work with the other side on behalf of the people.

❧

The nation was burdened with an $83 million debt when he came into office. With the help of his Secretary of the Treasury Albert Gallatin, he set about dismantling Hamilton's fiscal system and tried to disassemble the national bank. He eliminated a tax on whiskey, closed what he called "*unneces-*

sary offices" and reduced the Navy on the grounds that it wasn't needed in peacetime. He turned the Navy into a fleet of cheap gunboats that were useful only in defense, believing that this would not provoke any hostility from foreign powers. By the end of his second term, he had reduced the debt from $83 million to $57 million.

෯෪෫

Jefferson oversaw the establishment of the United States Military Academy at West Point, which was founded on March 16, 1802, as part of the Military Peace Establishment Act. The Act also established new laws and limits for the military, bringing it firmly under the control of the civilian government. In 1805, the Jay Treaty expired, and he did nothing to renew it. He also pardoned a number of people who had been imprisoned under the Alien and Sedition Acts.

FIRST BARBARY WAR

᷎᷎᷎

The Barbary States were nominally provinces of the Ottoman Empire, but they were independent countries. Tripoli, Algiers, Tunis and the Sultanate of Morocco fell under this umbrella title. The Barbary Coast of North Africa was rife with pirates, who were the scourge of the Mediterranean. It was estimated that from the 16th through the 19th centuries, the Barbary pirates kidnapped and enslaved some 1.25 million European citizens.

᷎᷎᷎

While the States were still colonies, American shipping in the Mediterranean was protected from these pirates by the Royal Navy. These protections obviously fell away after independence, and as a result, the pirates began to attack American shipping. They captured American merchant ships, pillaged the goods in their holds, and kidnapped the crews, whom they later either ransomed or sold as slaves.

❧

The first American ship to be attacked by the Barbary pirates was the *Betsey,* which was seized in October 1784. The Spanish government intervened and negotiated the release of the American men who had been taken a prisoner, and they advised the American government to pay tribute to the pirates in return for a cessation of future raids.

❧

In 1785, Algerian pirates captured the American ships, *Maria* and *Dauphin*, enslaving 115 American sailors. Each of the four Barbary States demanded $600,000 for the release of the men. Unfortunately, the maximum budget that the American envoys had at that time was $40,000 to split among the Barbary States. Diplomacy failed to achieve any success, and the crews of these ships were to spend an entire decade in chains.

❧

While he was still Minister to France, Jefferson sent envoys to Morocco and Algeria to attempt to negotiate treaties. Morocco signed a treaty with the United States on June 23, 1786, the first Barbary State to do so. Under that treaty, all piracy against American vessels was to cease, and any Americans captured by any of the Barbary States would be set free if they were to dock in any Moroccan city, to be protected by the Moroccan state. It was a diplomatic success.

❧

Algeria was more of a problem. They were not interested in

ending their raids on American shipping. Jefferson and John Adams traveled to London in 1786 to negotiate with Tripoli's representative, Sidi Haji Abdrahaman. Abdrahaman stated that the Koran required all followers of the Prophet to plunder and enslave all people who were sinners, which, as non-Muslims, the American sailors were. The only solution, he advised, was more tribute. In 1795, Algeria offered to release the 115 American sailors in return for a tribute payment of $1 million, which at that time was fully one-sixth of the entire budget of the United States.

🕉️

Jefferson argued, and many came to agree, that giving in to the Barbary States' demands would only encourage the pirates to push for more tribute in the future. The United States Department of the Navy was created by an act of Congress in 1798. Just before Jefferson's inauguration, Congress passed an addendum that put six frigates under the direction of the President. These ships were to

> *"protect our commerce and chastise their (the Barbary States')*
> *insolence – by sinking, burning or destroying their ships*
> *and vessels wherever you shall find them."*

🕉️

After Jefferson was sworn in, Yusuf Karamanli, the Pasha of Tripoli, demanded $225,000 in tribute from the new administration. Jefferson refused. In retaliation, the Pasha declared war on the United States by cutting down the flagstaff in front of the U. S. Consulate in Tripoli. Algiers and Tunis did not join Tripoli in its declaration of war, and Morocco continued to abide by its earlier treaty with the Americans.

❧

In 1801, Jefferson ordered the United States Navy under Commodore Richard Dale to travel to the Mediterranean to make a show of force. This was the first time an American naval squadron crossed the Atlantic. The fleet engaged with the Barbary pirates, and after this first violent contact, Jefferson sought and was granted a declaration of war from Congress. It was the first foreign war fought by the United States.

❧

Commodore Dale's fleet joined a Swedish fleet that was already blockading Tripoli, and the USS *Enterprise* vanquished the Barbary ship *Tripoli* in August 1801.

❧

The Pasha of Tripoli, Yusuf Karamanli, allowed and possibly ordered a group of Barbary pirates to capture the USS *Philadelphia*. The United States Marines were able to take the ship back in a daring night raid. Jefferson sent the United States' Consul to Tunis, William Eaton, with a military force to topple Yusuf and place his brother on the throne. Eaton and a force of US Marines and 500 mercenaries marched from Alexandria, Egypt to Tripoli, where they captured the city of Derna. This victory was the first time the flag of the United States was raised on foreign soil.

❧

With the threat of further military incursion by the Americans, and with the American blockade and bombardment of his city wearing his people down, Pasha Yusuf signed a peace treaty with the United States that restored peace to the Mediterranean, albeit temporarily. The people of the United States were overjoyed with the victory, and a monument was raised in the Washington Navy Yard. The Marine's Hymn includes a line about the shores of Tripoli in honor of the exploit.

LOUISIANA PURCHASE

❦

In 1800, Spain ceded its ownership of the Louisiana territory to France. At the time, France was ruled by Napoleon Bonaparte, and Napoleon's interest in his new property posed a potential security risk to shipping on the Mississippi River and the United States as a whole.

❦

At Jefferson's behest, James Monroe and Robert Livingston went to Paris in 1803 to negotiate for the purchase of New Orleans and its adjacent coastal region, thereby placing the mouth of the Mississippi River firmly in American hands. Jefferson offered $10 million for a tract of land that was roughly 40,000 square miles.

❦

Much to the surprise of Monroe and Livingston, Napoleon

made a generous counteroffer. Realizing that his military had no way to hold such a large expanse of land and needing money to continue to prosecute his wars in Europe, the French leader offered to sell nearly 828,000 square miles of land for $15 million. This land purchase would effectively double the size of the United States. With limited time and communication across the Atlantic being such a lengthy proposition, the negotiators accepted Napoleon's offer and signed the treaty of sale on April 30, 1803.

❧

Jefferson learned of his purchase on July 3, 1803. Although there were some concerns about the constitutionality of the federal government purchasing land, the Senate nevertheless voted to ratify the treaty on October 3, 1803.

❧

There was great optimism about the purchase, and the land that was obtained turned out to be incredibly fertile, making the new nation self-sufficient in foodstuffs and other resources for the first time. The purchase also ended British and French military incursions into North America, and the way was opened for the westward expansion of the United States to begin.

EXPEDITIONS

❧

J efferson knew that it was only a matter of time before
settlers started pushing west into the new territory, and
he wanted to know what he'd just bought. He also
wanted to state a claim to the rumored Northwest
Passage for the United States, hoping to head off the
European powers who were seeking the same thing. Armed
with the exploration accounts of Le Page du Pratz in
Louisiana, published in 1763, he convinced Congress to fund
an expedition to explore the continent all the way out to the
Pacific Ocean.

❧

The Corps of Discovery was founded in 1803, and Jefferson
tapped Merriweather Lewis and William Clark to be its leaders. He personally tutored Lewis on mapping, botany, natural
history, mineralogy, astronomy, and navigation. He gave Lewis
unlimited access to the library at Monticello, which at the

time boasted the largest collection of books in the world on the natural history and geography of North America. He also had a sizeable collection of maps, which Lewis obviously found to be of great value.

⚜

The Lewis and Clark Expedition lasted from May 1804 to September 1806 and returned with a wealth of information about the continent, significantly expanding knowledge and understanding of the geography, resources, and Native peoples of the land.

⚜

Lewis and Clark were not the only explorers that Jefferson sent westward. He also sent William Dunbar and George Hunter to the Ouachita River in Arkansas and Louisiana; Thomas Freeman and Peter Custis to the Red River; and Zebulon Pike to the Rocky Mountains and the Southwest. Every expedition brought back valuable information, much to the delight of the eternally intellectually curious Jefferson.

NATIVE AMERICAN POLICIES

৬২৯

Jefferson's attitude toward Native Americans was as conflicted as his attitude toward blacks. He openly disputed with the popularly held belief that indigenous people were inferior to those of European descent, and he believed that they were in fact equal "*in body and mind*" to whites. That is where his magnanimity ended.

৬২৯

As governor of Virginia, he advocated forcibly relocating the Cherokee and Shawnee tribes west of the Mississippi, allegedly because these tribes had supported the British during the Revolution. Once he became President, he arranged for Georgia to give up the lands it had claimed in the west in exchange for federal military assistance in clearing the Cherokee out of the state.

৬২৯

He believed in assimilation and sought to "*civilize*" the Native Americans. He attempted to secure peace treaties with the tribes that encouraged them to adopt the American agricultural lifestyle and to relinquish their old ways. Many tribes accepted his proposal, but some opposed it. The Shawnee tribe split into two factions over the issue, with the side led by Black Hoof agreeing to Jefferson's policies and the other side, led by Tecumseh, actively and violently opposing them. Jefferson told Secretary of War General Henry Dearborn,

"If we are constrained to lift the hatchet against any tribe, we will never lay it down until that tribe is exterminated or driven beyond the Mississippi."

❧ VI ❧
SECOND TERM

"Our country is now taking so steady a course as to show by what road it will pass to destruction, to wit: by consolidation of power first, and then corruption, its necessary consequence."

— THOMAS JEFFERSON

❧

Jefferson replaced Aaron Burr as his vice presidential candidate when he ran for re-election in 1804. His new running mate was George Clinton. Jefferson's relationship with Burr had been severely eroded by the outcome of the 1800 election, and Jefferson never stopped suspecting that Burr wanted the presidency for himself. In order to prevent Burr from gaining any sort of power base in Washington, Jefferson refused to appoint Burr's supporters to federal office, which infuriated Burr and opened a rift between them that would not heal.

CHALLENGES

❧

As soon as Jefferson was sworn in for his second term, he became involved in a political fracas with Supreme Court Justice Samuel Chase. Chase was a staunch Federalist, and he was unabashed in ruling in favor of his political allies. Jefferson determined to remove all Federalists from the bench, and he began by encouraging Congress to impeach Justice Chase. Virginia Congressman John Randolph and the House of Representatives served Chase with eight articles of impeachment based upon his judicial performance. The impeachment trial began in the Senate in 1805. Ultimately Chase was acquitted, Jefferson earned a permanent enemy in the form of Chief Justice John Marshall, and the proceedings raised constitutional questions regarding the independence of the judiciary. Although Chase was not convicted, his impeachment still helped to cement the idea that judges were prohibited from actively issuing rulings to further their partisan politics.

৩✿৩

The Republican party suffered a serious rupture in March 1806, when fellow Virginian John Randolph accused Jefferson on the floor of the House of moving too far in a Federalist direction, betraying their party's political base. The split was hurtful, because Randolph was Jefferson's second cousin, and he had previously been a staunch ally. In 1808, Randolph and his companions found an extra reason to be alarmed when Jefferson became the first president to push for a federal building project aimed at constructing roads, bridges, and canals across several states.

৩✿৩

Jefferson's popularity also was damaged by his response to events in Europe. He had a personal dislike for the British envoy, Anthony Merry, and this led to an erosion of previously positive relations between the two countries. Napoleon was waging a war of conquest in Europe, and after his victory at the Battle of Austerlitz, he unilaterally changed the terms of France's trade deals with the United States, and Jefferson's administration failed to counter these changes. Jefferson's response was the Embargo Act of 1807, which was aimed at goods from both France and Great Britain, but the end result was economic chaos at home. He abandoned the policy less than a year later.

৩✿৩

The states had abolished the international slave trade during the revolution, but South Carolina reopened in 1806. Jefferson decried this action in a December 1806 speech, calling on Congress to criminalize the international slave trade through federal legislation. In accordance with his wishes, Congress passed the Act Prohibiting Importation of Slaves, which Jefferson signed into law in 1807. The act barred international slave trading, but it did nothing to address the trade within the United States.

AARON BURR

❦

In 1804, shortly after he was dumped from the Democratic-Republican ticket, Aaron Burr suffered a drubbing at the polls when he ran for governor of New York. During the campaign, Alexander Hamilton had made inflammatory comments in public about the nature of Burr's character, and so Burr challenged Hamilton to a duel. On July 11, 1804, Burr shot and killed Hamilton. He was indicted for murder in New York and New Jersey, so he fled to Georgia. At about the same time, he was approached by New England separatists who wanted him to lead them in a New England Federation. They quickly distanced themselves from Burr after Hamilton's demise, and the still-sitting vice president's reputation and business dealings suffered. Looking for a way to improve his lot, he approached British ambassador Anthony Merry and offered to capture territory in the western United States in return for money and British ships.

❦

After his term as vice president ended, Burr traveled to Louisiana and began to conspire with the territorial governor, James Wilkinson. They began to recruit for a military expedition with the help of additional conspirators Senator John Smith of Ohio and an Irishman named Harmon Blennerhassett. During this time period, Burr floated a number of ideas that ranged from having New Orleans secede to create its state to invading and conquering Mexico or Spanish Florida. The ideas he came up with were many and varied, and to this day, nobody really knows what his goal really was.

⚜

In Fall 1806, Burr and a flotilla of ships with approximately sixty men set sail down the Ohio River toward New Orleans. At this point, Governor Wilkinson turned on him and reported Burr's activities to Jefferson, who immediately ordered his arrest. Burr was finally caught in Bayou Pierre, a wild area in Louisiana, and on February 13, 1807, he was sent to Virginia to stand trial for treason.

⚜

Burr's trial was a circus. Jefferson tried to influence the verdict by proclaiming Burr's obvious guilt in a speech before Congress. When the case actually came to trial, the judge was John Marshall, the Supreme Court Justice who was a political foe of Jefferson's, and he dismissed all charges. Burr's lawyers attempted to subpoena Jefferson to testify, but he invoked executive privilege and refused. This was the first exercise of executive privilege in the American presidency.

⚜

The trial lasted for three months, ultimately resulting in Burr's acquittal. Jefferson was furious and denounced the verdict. He removed Wilkinson from his position as governor but permitted him to retain his military commission.

THE CHESAPEAKE-LEOPARD
AFFAIR

৯৯৯

Throughout 1806 and 1807, the British Navy's press gangs busily raided American merchant ships and press-ganged their crews into service with the Royal Navy. Diplomacy did nothing to stop the impressment of American sailors, and Britain continued to harass American shipping.

৯৯৯

In June 1807, the HMS *Leopard* hailed the USS *Chesapeake* off the coast of Virginia. The commander of the American vessel, Commodore James Barron, accepted Lieutenant John Meade from the *Leopard*, and upon his arrival, Meade served Barron with a search warrant. The British, he claimed, were looking for deserters from the Royal Navy. After a brief discussion, Meade returned to the *Leopard*, and British Captain Humphreys demanded that the Americans surrender. The Americans declined, and the *Leopard* fired broadsides into the *Chesapeake*. Three of the crew were killed, and 18 were injured, including Barron. Completely unprepared for battle, Barron had no choice but to surrender. Humphreys refused the capitulation and boarded the *Chesapeake*, seizing four Royal Navy deserters, three of whom were American citizens. The British citizen was hanged from the yardarm of the HMS *Halifax*, and the three Americans were sentenced to 500 lashes each. The sentences were commuted.

⚜

Jefferson was furious. He issued a proclamation banning British ships from American waters and called on the states to call up 100,000 men and the materiel to arm them. The USS *Revenge* was sent to demand an explanation from the British government, but when it, too, was fired upon, Jefferson called a special session of Congress to discuss either an embargo of British goods or a declaration of war.

⚜

In December, Napoleon announced an embargo of British goods, preventing Britain from legally conducting any commerce in Europe, which was largely under Napoleon's control at that time. In response, George III ordered the impressment of American sailors to be intensified. Congress, in turn, passed the Embargo Act, which prohibited all British goods.

⚜

The embargo was not what one might call a success. The American economy suffered, and smugglers and scofflaws began to sell British goods at high prices on the black market.

Jefferson sent federal agents to track down and apprehend these smugglers. There was no real way to prevent American merchants from importing foreign goods, especially since they could just sail into international waters to conduct their business, but exports were sharply curtailed. The embargo failed.

❧

Another unintended consequence of the Embargo Act was Jefferson, who had always been against centralization of power, found himself expanding federal authority at the expense of the states. It was an untenable position politically, and the economic difficulties caused by the embargo helped to return the Federalists to power.

❧

In December 1807, Jefferson announced that he had no intention of seeking a third term and he retired to Monticello. Although he was still President, he left the actual affairs of state and business of running the country almost entirely to James Madison and Treasury Secretary Gallatin. Just before he left office in 1809, Jefferson repealed the disastrous embargo.

❧

Shortly after Madison's inauguration as his successor, Jefferson said that he felt like a prisoner who had been released from his chains.

❧ VII ❧
RETURN TO PRIVATE
LIFE

"I tremble for my country when I reflect that God I just; that his justice cannot sleep forever."

— THOMAS JEFFERSON

❧

During the years immediately after his time as President ended, Jefferson turned to his first love: education and learning. He sold his extensive book collection to the Library of Congress and began to correspond with the country's leaders. He advised James Monroe on westward expansion, and many see Jefferson's fingerprints on the famous Monroe Doctrine of 1823.

❧

Jefferson happily developed a routine. He would rise early, spend several hours reading and writing his copious correspondence, and in the afternoon he would oversee his plantation from horseback. In the evenings, he would spend time with his family in the garden, and then go to bed late at night with a book. He would have been happy to live his life just this way, with only his family around him, but his peace and quiet was frequently interrupted by visitors and even tourists who called without warning. He complained that Monticello had become a *"virtual hotel,"* but he never turned anyone away.

UNIVERSITY OF VIRGINIA

❧

J efferson had never been a religious man, and he believed that the key to a successful society was education without the interference or influence of any church. He wanted a university where students from all walks of life could study any topic they chose, where their studies would be publicly funded, and they could enroll based on ability rather than social class or wealth.

❧

In 1819, at the age of 70, Jefferson founded the University of Virginia. He organized a campaign in the state legislature for its charter, and he purchased the land for the university with the assistance of Edmund Bacon. He designed most of the buildings, planned the curriculum, and acted as the school's first rector when the university opened its doors in 1825.

❧

Like most of Jefferson's architecture, the buildings at the University of Virginia were based on Greek and Roman structures. The university library, called the Rotunda, was based upon the Roman Pantheon, and each academic unit was designed with a two-story façade in the form of a columned Greek temple. The Rotunda was the center of the campus, which was a controversial thing at the time – all other universities were centered on churches. The university was always meant to be a secular institution.

❦

The standard university education at that time had three possible areas of focus: medicine, law or divinity. Under the Jefferson's direction, the University of Virginia had eight separate and independent schools: medicine, law, mathematics, chemistry, ancient languages, modern languages, natural philosophy and moral philosophy. These were all areas where Jefferson himself was skilled.

❦

Jefferson hosted dinners at Monticello on Sundays for faculty and students for the rest of his life. When Jefferson passed away, he bequeathed the majority of his library to the university.

JEFFERSON AND ADAMS

❧

There have rarely been two politicians as entwined throughout their careers as Thomas Jefferson and John Adams. They began as good friends when they served in the Continental Congress together and then again when they represented the United States' interests in Europe. Party politics shattered their friendship, and after Jefferson's election to the presidency, the two men were not on speaking terms for more than ten years.

❧

In 1804, when Jefferson's daughter Polly passed away, Abigail Adams wrote to Jefferson and attempted to arrange reconciliation, but when the men did write to one another again, their old arguments flared up, and they became hostile once more.

❧

Benjamin Rush, another signer of the Declaration of Independence, was dedicated to healing the rift between the two men. He prodded them continually to contact one another, and his efforts combined with the passage of time led to Adams sending a New Year's letter to Jefferson. Jefferson responded with warmth, which prompted Adams to write back. The two began a 14-year correspondence during which they exchanged 158 letters debating politics, history, and the impact of the American revolution on the world.

꧁꧂

When Adams died, his last words were, "**_Thomas Jefferson survives._**" Unfortunately, in an extraordinary coincidence, Jefferson had actually died a few hours before.

AUTOBIOGRAPHY

&

In 1821, when he was 77 years old, Jefferson put pen to paper and began writing an autobiography. He focused exclusively on the years of the revolution, excluding his boyhood and youth. He wrote about nothing that happened after July 29, 1790.

&

Jefferson had never been particularly interested in his family history, but he did write that his family had come to the New World from Wales, settling in Virginia in the late 17th Century. He described his father as a good man with a strong mind and sound judgment despite the fact that he was uneducated. After these basic sketches, he concentrated on the Declaration of Independence and the establishment of the state government of Virginia.

&

He took the opportunity to express his opinions and insights about human nature, politics, and historical events. He decried the aristocracy of landowners, saying that he would rather see an aristocracy of talent and virtue. Jefferson also stated that he felt his personal affairs were unimportant and best if overlooked.

LAFAYETTE

❧

W hen he left Paris in 1789, Jefferson had parted from his good friend the Marquis de Lafayette. The two had written to one another, but they had not seen each other in many, many years. In 1824, Lafayette accepted an invitation from President James Monroe to visit the United States to see what he had helped to create. He visited New York, New England, and Washington, but when his official visits were done, Lafayette went to Monticello.

❧

The visit was an emotional one for them both. Jefferson's grandson, Randolph, described how the two men burst into tears and embraced when they saw one another. Lafayette stayed at Monticello for 11 days, during which he, Jefferson and President Monroe toured the University of Virginia and attended a banquet. Jefferson had prepared a speech for the occasion, but his voice was weak, so he had someone else read it for him. It was his last public appearance.

SUNSET

❧

I n his final years, Jefferson was deeply indebted, to the tune of $100,000. He worried about making good on this debt, especially as he realized that his life was coming to an end and he would have little to leave to his heirs. He applied to the General Assembly of Virginia to hold a public lottery as a fundraiser, and the Assembly consented.

❧

His health began to fail in 1825, a combination of disorders of the intestines and urinary tract, rheumatism, and old and painful injuries of the wrist and arms. He was confined to bed in June 1826, and on July 4, at 12:50 pm, Jefferson died at the age of 83. The date of his death was the 50th anniversary of the Declaration of Independence, and it was also, as previously mentioned, the date of John Adams' demise.

❧

When he died, a golden locket was found around Jefferson's neck. It contained a lock of his wife Martha's hair, bound by a faded blue ribbon.

৩৯৫

At the time of his death, Jefferson was still deeply in debt, and though he left instructions for the disposition of his estate and the emancipation of Sally Hemings' children, the estate was sold at public auction in 1827. His possessions and slaves were all sold to pay off his expenses, and in 1831, his heirs sold Monticello.

❧ VIII ☙
LEGACY

"When a man assumes a public trust, he should consider himself a public property."

— THOMAS JEFFERSON

❧

Thomas Jefferson was one of the most influential political philosophers of his day. He had marked opinions, and his persuasive writing ensured that his influence would continue to be felt long after his death.

GOVERNMENT

❧

His vision of government based upon ideals of political equality is known as *"Jeffersonian democracy."* Jefferson strongly believed that each individual was born with *"certain inalienable rights,"* which included liberty up until the moment that liberty infringed on the rights of others. He was also a staunch supporter of the separation of church and state. He distrusted cities and bankers, and he believed that tyranny was an outgrowth of corruption in politics and monarchies. He was opposed to centralization of power, which informed his support for states' rights.

❧

At the time of his death, the United States was the only existing republic in an age of monarchies. Jefferson was a tireless opponent of monarchies and hereditary power, and he opined that frequent small outbreaks of rebellion and revolution were necessary to keep monarchies, governments and other powerful entities in check. He believed that the majority of human history was a tale of a majority oppressed by a powerful minority, and he believed in democracy as pure majority rule.

※

Jefferson believed in public education and freedom of the press. He also supported the idea of providing the vote not just to landholders but also to laborers who did not own land. He wanted to increase voter participation, and while his party was in power, this did indeed happen. He was displeased that the vote was largely in the hands of rich and powerful landowners, believing that this was an echo of the feudal system of monarchy. He wanted to expand suffrage to include "*yeoman farmers*," but he excluded tenant farmers, day laborers, vagrants, most Native Americans, and women. It was his belief that voting should be restricted only to those people who were free of outside influences and corrupting dependence on other people or institutions.

※

While he was a firm believer in democracy, he realized that there would be times when there would be failures or excesses. These would be the fault of corrupt institutions rather than the foibles of human nature, which separated him from some of his more cynical compatriots who doubted if human beings could be trusted to govern themselves.

RELIGION

☙❧

J efferson was baptized into the Episcopal Church, but after being influenced by Deists and studying the New Testament on his own, he broke from traditional Christianity. He called himself a Christian,

"in the only sense in which Jesus wished anyone to be."

He compiled all of Jesus's words and teachings, omitting all references to the miracles or the supernatural, and created *The Life and Morals of Jesus of Nazareth*, which is known today as the *Jefferson Bible*.

☙❧

He strongly disliked priests and clergy of all kinds, and he toyed with the idea of banning all members of the clergy from public office. He believed that the clergy, dedicated to the hierarchies of their respective churches, were the enemies of liberty and discouraged individual liberty in favor of conformity. He drafted the Virginia Statute of Religious Freedom, which was ratified in 1786, and he was so proud of this accomplishment that it was only one of his voluminous writings to be included in the epitaph he wrote for his gravestone.

❦

Jefferson hoped that the American people would be educated in multiple faiths and would create an "*Apiarian*" religion, which meant that the people would rationally take the best features of every religion and discard the rest. He believed in a Creator and an afterlife, but he denied the divinity of Jesus and rejected the concept of the Trinity. These beliefs were extremely controversial in their time, and they featured strongly in opposition to his election for a second term as President.

❦

During the campaign for the 1800 election, the *New England Palladium* referred to Jefferson as an "*infidel*," and the Federalists called him a "*howling atheist.*" He never denied the existence of or his belief in God, but the opposition to his views that he experienced during that campaign led him to become more reticent to discuss his beliefs in public.

BANKS

✿

He was always a farmer at heart, and he believed that agrarian citizens were hurt in the long run by government banks and public borrowing. He believed that such institutions encouraged risk-taking, long-term debt, monopolies and dangerous financial speculation. He disliked Alexander Hamilton primarily because his rival was a staunch supporter of a national bank, and that friction was the seed of all the acrimony between them.

✿

Jefferson and Madison both felt that a national bank would be neglectful to the needs of individuals and farmers. Jefferson also believed that the foundation of a national bank would violate the Tenth Amendment and would be a violation of states' rights. He wanted to abolish the national bank when he became President, and only the efforts of Secretary of the

Treasury Albert Gallatin convinced him to let the bank remain.

SLAVERY

꧁

Thomas Jefferson was a slave owner, which was a dreadful contradiction for a man who so frequently stated his belief in personal liberty. Over his lifetime, he owned over 600 human beings. He inherited 175 of these people, and the rest were born into bondage on his plantations. While he may have been a benevolent slaveholder, the fact remains that he continually denied personal liberty to the people who worked his land while he sat in Monticello and wrote vaunted words about liberty and freedom.

꧁

He felt that slavery was harmful to everyone involved with it, both slave and master, but he never saw fit to distance himself from it completely. His personal wealth, based as it was on the plantation system, depended upon slave labor to be maintained. At the same time, he frequently included verbiage highly critical to the institution of slavery in his writings. Passages calling for the abolition of slavery were included in, but later struck from, the Declaration of Independence.

❦

He believed, as many white men of his time did, that blacks were inherently inferior to whites both mentally and physically. Despite this, he also believed that they had innate rights that should not be violated. In *Notes on the State of Virginia*, he called slavery a moral evil and stated that the United States would one day be called to account by God. He supported freeing slaves, but immediately deporting them to Liberia or Sierra Leone. He did not believe that whites and blacks could live together as free members of the same society, and following the slave revolt in Haiti, he feared a race war in America.

❦

Jefferson was allegedly a benevolent slaveholder. He purchased slaves to reunite families, but he also sold about 110 slaves to obtain funds. By the standards of the day, he didn't force his slaves to work on Sundays or Christmas, and he allowed them personal time during the winter. He provided them with log cabins with fireplaces, good, clothing and household goods, and he gave them financial incentives for jobs well done. He also allowed them to raise their chickens and to grow gardens. His nail factory was operated by child slaves, but these same slaves went on to become craftsmen, and he frequently promoted slaves to better positions on the plantation.

Benevolence as a slaveholder, however, is still an offense to the personhood and liberty of the slave, and in a way, saying Jefferson was a "*good master*" is damning with faint praise.

THE SALLY HEMINGS QUESTION

❧

I n 1802, a man named James Callender was denied the position of postmaster. He immediately retaliated by proclaiming in public that Jefferson had taken slave Sally Hemings as "*a concubine*" and that she had borne him several children. This allegation was dismissed by polite society, but it was an open secret that many slave owners had children with women they enslaved.

❧

Sally Hemings was the daughter of John Wayles, Jefferson's father-in-law, and Betty Hemings, Wayles "*mulatto*" slave. She was his wife Martha's half-sister and was three-quarters European and one-quarter African.

❧

Jefferson's family denied the relationship, but visitors to

Monticello often remarked on the close resemblance of the Hemings children to Jefferson himself. Randolph Jefferson, Thomas's grandson, once claimed that the last Peter Carr, Jefferson's nephew by his sister, had fired Hemings' children, but this claim was never credited.

୭ୡୠୡ

In 1794, Jefferson freed his slave Robert Hemings, and in 1796, he also freed James Hemings, who was his cook. A slave named Harriet Hemings was freed in 1822 when she tried to run away, and in his will, he freed five more male slaves named Hemings.

୭ୡୠୡ

Sally had four children who survived to adulthood: William Beverly, Harriet, Madison and Eston Hemings. All but Madison identified themselves as white and lived in white communities. In 1873, Madison Hemings went on record in an Ohio newspaper stating that Jefferson was his father. He claimed that all of his siblings were Jefferson's children, and that claim was backed by Israel Jefferson, another freed slave who had worked at Monticello. Madison was dismissed as a liar.

୭ୡୠୡ

The rumor would not go away, something that plagued Jefferson's descendants. Mainstream historians gave no credence to the story, but African-American historians kept the story alive. Finally, in 1998, a DNA study was conducted on the Y-chromosome of a direct male-line descendant of Eston Hemings. It was found to be a nearly perfect match to descendants of Jefferson's paternal uncle. Peter Carr's descendants were not a match to the Hemings sample. The results of this test were interpreted as stating with 99% certainty that Jefferson was indeed the father of Sally Hemings' children.

❧

In July 2017, the Thomas Jefferson Foundation announced that archaeologists who were excavating at Monticello had located what they believed were Sally Hemings' quarters, adjacent to Jefferson's bedchamber. This chamber has been preserved as part of the Mountaintop Project, which is dedicated to the restoration of Monticello. Tours of Monticello now include acknowledgment of Jefferson's relationship with Hemings.

❧

Sally Hemings was never emancipated. She was, however, permitted by Jefferson's daughter Patsy to live with her freed sons as a free woman in Charlottesville, Virginia. She died in 1835.

❧ IX ❧

THE MEASURE OF A MAN

"I was bold in the pursuit of knowledge, never fearing to follow truth and reason to whatever results they led, and bearding every authority which stood in their way."

— THOMAS JEFFERSON

❧

Thomas Jefferson is remembered today as an icon of personal liberty, democracy, republicanism and as one of the Founding Fathers whose efforts brought the United States into being. He was more than a politician, and his contributions to American society are nothing less than staggering.

❧

He was a true Renaissance man. He was a member of the American Philosophical Society for 35 years and served as the president of that organization for 18 years. He was a scientist, fascinated by the development of new crops and scientific agricultural techniques. He was an architect who helped to promote the popularity of neo-classical and Neo-Palladian architectural forms. He was a prodigious writer, a linguist who mastered several languages, and a naturalist who studied birds, wine, natural bridges and soil conditions. He designed gardens and invented the swivel chair, the prototype of which he used while he was writing the Declaration of Independence. He improved many contemporary inventions, adapting them to his needs. These inventions included the pedometer, the polygraph (not the lie detector, but a device that duplicated writing), the revolving bookcase and a form of plow called the moldboard plow.

৩৵৩

His strong support of states' rights caused him to lose popularity during the Civil War years, and his contradictory record on human rights, particularly slavery, have dimmed his luster over the years. Despite this, he was named as the fifth greatest President the country ever had in a 2015 Brookings Institution poll of the American Political Science Association.

৩৵৩

Thomas Jefferson was a complex individual, with good qualities and bad qualities, as most people have. His accomplishments may be blemished by his failings, but he stands out as one of the most remarkable men of his day.

❧ X ❧

BIBLIOGRAPHY

❧❧

- Bernstein, Richard B. (2003). *Thomas Jefferson*.
  Oxford University Press. ISBN 978-0195181302.
- Bober, Natalie (2008). *Thomas Jefferson: Draftsman
  of a Nation*. University of Virginia Press. ISBN 978-
  0813927329.
- Cogliano, Francis D (2008). *Thomas Jefferson:
  Reputation and Legacy*. Edinburgh University Press.
  ISBN 978-0748624997.
- Meacham, Jon (2012). *Thomas Jefferson: The Art of
  Power*. Random House LLC. ISBN 978-
  0679645368.
- Randall, Willard Sterne (1994). *Thomas Jefferson: A
  Life*. Harper Collins. ISBN 0060976179.

ALEXANDER HAMILTON

One of The Most Influential Founding
Fathers

❧ I ❧
THE ORPHAN OF THE CARIBBEAN

"A promise must never be broken."

— ALEXANDER HAMILTON

❦

Alexander Hamilton started his life in the British West Indies and would grow to become one of the most influential Founding Fathers of the United States. For many Americans, his story seems like a classic tale from rags to riches, of a poor boy whose hard work and perseverance allowed him to become one of the greatest historical figures of a nation. This popular perception is recent, caused by the explosive success of Lin-Manuel Miranda's Broadway show *Hamilton: An American Musical*, which spread across the globe like wildfire. The truth is not as pretty, certainly not neat, and not as politically correct as the musical, but that makes it no less interesting and instead means there's a lot that the general public can learn from such a complex figure as Alexander Hamilton.

❧

Hamilton entered a world where both sides of the Atlantic Ocean were dominated by Europe and Great Britain in particular. The 18th century featured the gradual rise of Britain to global prominence through the strength of its navy and colonies. Britain not only owned the thirteen North American colonies that would become the United States later in the century, but it also possessed significant regions of the Caribbean, including the British West Indies. The Atlantic slave trade was in full swing, and white European landowners continued to be the top of society.

❧

Hamilton was born on January 11th, 1755 or 1757. Hamilton himself listed his birth year in 1757, but Dutch papers uncovered during the 1930s listed him as 13 years old in a probate document from St. Croix made in 1768. The document, drafted after the death of Hamilton's mother, might have the wrong age listed from an error on the part of the writer. Another theory is that the young, orphaned Alexander deliberately gave the wrong birthdate to appear older and therefore more employable since thirteen-year-old boys were eligible to enter apprenticeships. Whatever the case may be, historians know his parents to have been Rachel Faucette and James A. Hamilton.

❧

Rachel Faucette was a married woman who abandoned her original husband and children and traveled to St. Kitts in the British West Indies. However, she did have her reasons for leaving. Rachel had married a man by the name of John Lavien, an unsuccessful merchant when she was 16 and he 28. By all accounts, Lavien had done his best at pretending to be wealthy whilst arranging the marriage with Rachel's mother and quickly turned into an abusive man after the wedding when he found out that the Faucette family did not have money. When Rachel started to associate with other men, Lavien had her jailed as punishment despite his infidelity.

৬২৪৩

Eventually, Lavien decided to petition for her release, believing Rachel would be more docile and obey him. However, once out of jail, Rachel quickly packed up with her mother and left, making the trip to St. Kitts. While there, she met James Hamilton and commenced an affair. James Hamilton was a noble Scotsman, the fourth son of a Laird, or a Scottish noble with an established estate. The pair moved to Nevis in the Leeward Islands and had two children: James Jr. and Alexander. Eventually, the older James Hamilton abandoned Rachel and their children when he discovered that her original husband intended to divorce her for adultery and Rachel could then be charged with bigamy, a serious crime that would result in her return to prison. Although James seemed to remain in contact with Rachel and his sons, he did not offer any significant financial or emotional support to the family.

৬২৪৩

Rachel moved to Nevis because she inherited some property

in the region from her father in the capital city of Charlestown. However, she could not sustain herself and her children in the region and moved the family to St. Croix instead a little later. In St. Croix, she established a small store and ran it until her death from yellow fever in 1768. Her death did not bode well for Alexander, who suffered emotionally for years from the loss of his mother. To make matters worse, Rachel's official husband seized the shop and estate in probate court and auctioned off her possessions, keeping the money for himself. Alexander received only his mother's collection of books, which a family friend purchased at auction and returned to Alexander and his brother. Alexander's father once again did not appear to be in the picture and offered little support to his sons.

⚜

At the tender age of 13 (or 11), Hamilton became a clerk at an import-export firm called Beekman and Cruger, which frequently traded with the American colonies in New England or the northeastern section of the United States which includes places like New York and Massachusetts. He and his brother briefly lived with their cousin, an emotionally depressed man by the name of Peter Lytton. Unfortunately, in 1769, Lytton committed suicide and left all the property to his mistress and their son. James Jr. and Alexander found themselves separated as the older James left to work with a carpenter and Alexander found a home with a family friend, one Thomas Stevens.

⚜

During his time with the Stevens family, Hamilton continued to work in the trading industry and became friends with

Edward Stevens, Thomas's son with whom he shared many interests. He made a significant impression on his bosses and was deemed competent enough to be left in charge of the firm for five whole months in 1771 when the owner went to sea. At 15, the young Alexander Hamilton already showed more ambition and determination than many adults. Accounts indicate he already wanted to leave the British West Indies to pursue a life in an area with more opportunities.

⚜

Alexander's tenacity would serve him well since he was in a rare position. He could have opportunities if he tried, but he would need to work for them. Although he experienced a rough period following the death of his mother, Hamilton lived a privileged existence compared to other boys his age. Instead of being taken advantage of or sent to live on the streets, he and his brother were taken care of by family friends and obtained influential apprenticeships. His mother had owned at least two slaves, and the families Hamilton lived with also possessed slaves that took care of menial labor and the upkeep of the home. Even as an illegitimate child, Hamilton was given significant advantages that would set him up later in life.

⚜

Although the Church of England refused to admit Hamilton to the church school due to his parentage and the circumstances of his birth, he had received some private tutoring and schooling at an institute led by a Jewish headmistress. This schooling would have been considered enough for a boy of his social status, but Hamilton was not satisfied. He heavily supplemented this formal education with his innate love of reading and writing. Around 1771, Hamilton began to yearn for a life outside of the British West Indies but leaving would be no small feat. After all, even with his advantages, he was still a young orphan even if he was developing some success in the trading business. What he needed was someone who would be willing to not only get him off the islands but also offer a modicum of support in a new location. And this Hamilton received.

❧

In 1772, Hamilton wrote an elaborate and detailed letter to his father describing a massive hurricane which struck the island on August 30th of that same year. The letter, with its graphic descriptions and religious tones and themes, garnered the praise of one Hugh Knox, a minister, journalist, and acquaintance of the older James Hamilton. Knox published the letter in the ***Royal Danish-American Gazette***, where it, in turn, drew admiration from fervent readers. Several critics wrote in praising the sophisticated language and imagery, and community leaders collected a fund to send the intelligent clerk to the North American colonies for more formal education.

❧

In short, Hamilton earned his ticket out of the British West Indies with an essay.

THE NEW BOY IN
NEW YORK

"There is a certain enthusiasm in liberty, that makes
human nature rise above itself, in acts of bravery and
heroism."

— ALEXANDER HAMILTON

❧

The funds collected by community leaders were enough to
buy the teenaged Alexander Hamilton passage across the
Atlantic. He arrived in Boston sometime in October of 1772
and from there traveled to New York by stagecoach. While in
the city, he received lodging from one Hercules Mulligan, the
brother of a trader who had worked with the firm of
Beekman and Cruger. Mulligan worked with Hamilton to sell
cargo and goods that would go towards paying for Hamilton's

food, schooling, and other expenses while staying in the British colonies.

ॐ

Starting in 1773, Hamilton attended classes at the Elizabethtown Academy in New Jersey. His education in the British West Indies, because he had been banned from attending the church school, included many gaps that would be essential for college work. In particular, Hamilton needed to brush up on the popular subjects of the time, including rhetoric, geography, history, and French. While at a preparatory school, Hamilton associated with future revolutionary and politician William Livingston and even lived with him for a short period.

ॐ

That fall, Hamilton was able to attend King's College (the current Columbia University) as a private student before becoming fully matriculated in 1774. While there, Hamilton made numerous friends and acquaintances, among them many future revolutionaries. Indeed, looking at just who Hamilton lived and worked with during his formative teenage years, it's not surprising that he would grow to become one of the Union's most fervent supporters. Mulligan was a revolutionary and eventual spy during the war and Livingston already spent much of his time spouting new, revolutionary ideas against the British and King George. Records indicate that Hamilton's first public appearance included him concisely and succinctly explaining the position of many patriots, as they were known in the 1770s, at Liberty Pole.

ॐ

While in college, Hamilton and his friends additionally formed an unnamed literary society that would go on to become the famous Philolexian Society at Columbia University. He also developed some impressive writings during this time, fleshing out his political ideas and literary prowess. His first political writings, *A Full Vindication of the Measures of Congress* and *The Farmer Refuted*, appeared in 1774 when Hamilton responded to the work of loyalist and Church of England clergyman Samuel Seabury. Seabury wished to scare people away from the revolutionary cause and was writing to a large audience – what many modern individuals don't realize is that the thirteen colonies were not filled with people chomping at the bit for independence. At least 1/3 were Loyalists while another 1/3 just wanted to be left alone to live their lives in peace.

❦

Hamilton went on to author many more pieces that year, including two documents that targeted and attacked the Quebec Act of 1774. The Quebec Act was part of a series of British political acts lumped together and collectively known as the Intolerable or Coercive Acts by colonial patriots. Although targeted at the territory of Quebec, many patriots believed that the new political system contained within would soon be applied to the thirteen American colonies and that the colonies would lose their elected governments. It's also believed that Hamilton wrote fifteen anonymous installments of "*The Monitor*" in the *New York Journal* that same year.

❦

Despite being a fervent patriot, Hamilton proved himself to be a peaceful man off the battlefield. He condemned the mobs that went about attacking loyalists and even saved the loyalist president of his college in 1775. How? By orating to the crowd long enough for the president to slip away to a safe place. This calm and pacifism did not extend to the battle-field, though. During that same year, following the first engagement of American and British troops at Lexington and Concord, Hamilton and many other students from King's College joined a New York voluntary militia. Originally called the Corsicans, the company would be renamed the Hearts of Oak.

※

Hamilton regularly performed drills with the company before classes. The militia established its training area in a graveyard of a nearby chapel. They wore uniforms they designed them-selves: short green jackets, badges with red tin hearts and the motto "**God and Our Right**," and round leather hats with cockades (circles of ribbons) and the phrase "**Liberty or Death**" around the band. In his spare time, Hamilton studied military tactics and history and deliberately made use of this new knowledge during drills. Soon, his dedication and studies paid off, and his superiors in the militia recommended him for a promotion.

※

In August 1775, Hamilton received his first taste of combat when the Hearts of Oak received orders to raid the Battery and take possession of cannonry held inside. While under heavy fire from the British HMS Asia, Hamilton and his comrades successfully grabbed the equipment. The Hearts of Oak became an artillery unit afterward and were able to keep the cannonry.

⚜

Despite being a great student and doing well in his studies, Hamilton was forced to leave King's College in 1776 when the college shut down following the British occupation of the city. Hamilton remained a part of the militia and managed to attain the rank of captain after being promoted through his connections to patriots like John Jay and Alexander McDougall. Hamilton received a new task: gather forces to form the New York Provincial Company of Artillery. Through his efforts, he managed to gather together sixty men and was placed in charge of the company.

⚜

The New York Provincial Company of Artillery under Hamilton participated in the campaign of 1776 around New York City. He led them through the Battle of White Plains and the Battle of Trenton. During the Battle of Trenton, Hamilton stationed his soldiers at the intersection of Warren and Broad streets to keep hired German mercenaries trapped in the barracks and out of the main fighting. The maneuver was a success, and Hamilton went on to participate in the Battle of Princeton in January of 1777. Washington led the American forces and managed to beat the British back far enough that they took refuge in Nassau Hall. At this point, Hamilton brought out three cannons and commenced fire upon the Princeton College building, forcing a surrender out of the British.

Hamilton's time at school would not continue until after the American Revolution. Instead, he set his sights on a military career, believing that the glory it offered would be sufficient to carve out a place for himself in the new world approaching.

❧ III ❧

A REVOLUTIONARY FOR WASHINGTON

"I think the first duty of society is justice."

— ALEXANDER HAMILTON

❦

The desired military career did not start the way Hamilton expected. He received offers to become the aide to several influential generals, including William Alexander (Lord Stirling) and either Alexander McDougall or Nathanael Greene. He rejected both positions, striving to earn his glory in combat. However, he soon received one that he could not brush aside: a request from General George Washington to become one of his own aides de camp. Seeing as how Washington was the leader of the Continental Army, it would have been political and social suicide to decline.

Hamilton then became Washington's chief staff aide in 1777 with the rank of lieutenant colonel, a position he would retain for four entire years. Because he was an educated man and an eloquent writer, Hamilton became responsible for recording many of Washington's letters and correspondences, including documents sent to Congress, state governors, and the other military personnel in the Continental Army. Soon, he even issued orders dictated by Washington but signed with his name. His role as one of Washington's aides additionally put him on the path where he would meet his wife, Elizabeth Schuyler.

Elizabeth (Eliza) Schuyler was the middle child of the wealthy General Philip Schuyler. By all accounts, she possessed a fiery and impulsive personality tempered by her desire to help others. She met Alexander Hamilton when she was 23 years old in Morristown, New Jersey. The pair hit it off immediately and exchanged letters for a single month before becoming engaged. Hamilton seemed particularly infatuated with Elizabeth, although many of his detractors believed he married her for the fortune he received after the wedding. The two spend a brief honeymoon together in 1780 before Hamilton returned to his military duties. Their first child, Philip, was born less than a year later and would be one of eight over the next 24 years.

While serving as the chief staff aide, Hamilton became involved in other high-level intrigue and administration, including diplomacy, intelligence, and negotiations with other senior officers in the army. He even formed lasting friendships with important figures like the Marquis de Lafayette and John Laurens. However, he continued to desire active combat and another military command of his own, one that he would have more freedom to run since he had been given such a high rank. Around 1781, as the war quickly drew to a close, Hamilton became frantic.

In February, he used a slight reprimand from Washington as the excuse he needed to resign from his staff position. He began to petition for and request a field command, going so far as to send a letter to Washington with his commission – papers that made him an officer – enclosed in July. By the end of the month, Washington relented. Hamilton received a new commission as a commander of the light infantry companies from the 1st and 2nd New York Regiments and two more provisional companies that came north from Connecticut.

Hamilton even got his chance to see combat by participating in the final major military operation in North America during the Revolutionary War: The Battle of Yorktown. He was placed in charge of three battalions and ordered to fight with allied French troops to take two British fortifications around the city of Yorktown. Hamilton and his battalions managed to take one of the battalions in a nighttime action, fighting with bayonets at close quarters. The French, although they suffered heavy casualties, also took their target. The British, having lost their advantage over Yorktown, surrendered.

Following his success, Hamilton resigned from the Continental Army and set his sights on attending the Congress of the Confederation being held. He gained the appointment of a New York representative in July 1782, with his term beginning in November of that same year. This fit into Hamilton's plans nicely: In his letters, he already expressed his disappointment and frustration with how the wartime Continental Congress ran, in particular, its decentralization and need to receive financial support from the states on a voluntary basis. The Articles of Confederation which established the Congress in the first place could not collect taxes or other money from the states, meaning the federal government was weak and unable to garner the support it needed without full state cooperation.

Hamilton's first goal as a representative was to garner support for an amendment proposed by Thomas Burke that gave Congress the power to collect a 5% duty on imported goods from each of the states. The amendment had been proposed in 1781 but needed the support of all the states to be passed, and Rhode Island rejected it in November 1782. Hamilton worked together with James Madison to get a delegation together to send to Rhode Island and wrote an argument for them to present. The argument stated that the national government needed to retain some level of financial autonomy and had the ability to make laws that surpassed those of the states. However, Virginia soon took back its ratification of the amendment, and the delegation to Rhode Island was canceled.

However, Hamilton did not give up on his attempts to get money from the states. While he was a member of Congress, the disgruntled and frustrated soldiers of the Continental Army sent a delegation to Congress. Because the fledgling federal government had no way to raise revenue, it had no money to supply its soldiers and hadn't paid them in eight months. The officers from Valley Forge had been promised pensions they didn't receive. The delegation arrived before Congress led by one Captain Alexander McDougall and stated three demands. First, that the regular soldiers receive the wages owed them. Second, that the officers receive their pensions. Third, if the government could not afford to pay the pension for life, then it gives the money as a lump sum to the officers. Congress rejected the demands as it had no money.

Hamilton joined a group of Congressmen which encouraged MacDougall to be aggressive and threaten Congress with unknown consequences while simultaneously voting against any proposals that did not include general federal taxation. He did not want a temporary tax or the states to assume the military debts: He wanted federal taxation, only this time with representation. Hamilton wanted to use the discontented army for this purpose and wrote to several officers, suggesting they defy civil authority. Washington wrote to Hamilton and rebuked him, stating that it was dangerous to manipulate the military in such a way.

Washington eventually defused the situation by dealing with the officers personally and sending them on their way around March 15th. Congress disbanded the Continental Army in April 1783, ending the standing American military. At the same time, Congress created a 25-year tax or impost and suggested that the government turn the officers' pensions into five years of full pay instead of a lifetime of half pay. Both measures required the approval of all 13 states, and Rhode Island once again refused to support either measure. An angry Hamilton was viewed as excessive, but he soon had another chance to petition for a strong federal government.

❧

In June 1783, angry soldiers marched from Lancaster, Pennsylvania to Philadelphia, where Congress was held. Congress ordered Hamilton and two other former militia members to intercept the mob but gave them no reinforcements. Hamilton ordered the Secretary of War to try to intervene, but his maneuvers were unsuccessful. Finally, Hamilton suggested that the Congress move to Princeton, New Jersey to avoid the angry soldiers, which it did. While in Princeton, Hamilton drafted a new measure, this time to call for a revision of the weak Articles of Confederation that held the fledgling American government together. His resolution featured some aspects that would make their way into the current U.S. Constitution, including the separation of powers into the Legislative, Judicial, and Executive branches.

❧

Unfortunately, some time would pass before a revision of the Articles of Confederation came to fruition. Hamilton resigned from Congress and continued his studies during his personal time, eventually passing the legal bar and establishing his own practice in Albany, New York. He specialized in defending former loyalists – also called Tories – and damages done by British subjects during the war. He consistently made sure that legal judgments upheld the law established by the 1783 Treaty of Paris that ended the Revolutionary War and strived to follow the letter of the law as well as the spirit, demonstrating his fastidiousness and reverence for a strong, commanding government.

۞

While the issues of the federal government still plagued him, Hamilton focused on accomplishing some of his other goals. His fondness and sense of duty towards his former university encouraged Hamilton to restore King's College as Columbia College, ending its eight-year suspension and helping rebuild many of its destroyed halls. In 1784, Hamilton also founded one of the oldest banks in the United States: The Bank of New York. While working on these accomplishments, he assumed a leadership role in the Annapolis Convention of 1786, which was a political convention attended by twelve delegates from five states. The purpose was to discuss the weaknesses of the Articles of Confederation, which Hamilton did with gusto. He personally drafted the Convention's resolution to hold another constitutional convention, this time to create a stronger government.

❧ IV ❧

A COMMANDING CRITIC
AND A MAN OF THE
CONSTITUTION

"I never expect to see a perfect work from an
imperfect man."

— ALEXANDER HAMILTON

❧

In 1787, Hamilton was chosen to be an assemblyman representing New York County in the New York State Legislature.
He was also chosen to be a delegate for the Constitutional
Convention due to the support of his father-in-law, General
Schuyler. Even though Hamilton was a central figure in the
decision to call another Constitutional Convention, he failed
to be directly influential. New York had two other delegates
attending the event: Robert Yates and John Lansing Jr. Both
men represented Governor George Clinton of New York and

opposed the idea of a strong federal government, instead of petitioning for powerful state legislatures and a weak national government. The two men always voted in unison, ensuring none of Hamilton's changes to the Articles of Confederation could get through.

❧

While at the Convention, Hamilton managed to alienate many of the other attendees by giving a speech in which he proposed electing a President-for-Life. His idea was that the president and elected senators would hold their positions until they died or were removed for corruption or abuse of their power. Hamilton believed that the *"English model was the only good one on this subject"* and that a leader for life had a far more invested interest in the future and wellbeing of a nation than one who left office after a few years. His ideas did not go over well with revolutionaries like James Madison, who believed Hamilton was a not-so-secret monarchist attempting to bring back the very regime the colonies had fought to escape.

❧

By the time the Constitutional Convention ended, Hamilton was not happy with the results but thought the document was much better than the original Articles of Confederation. He signed it and convinced several of the other delegates to do so as well. By the end of the Convention, he was the only member of the New York delegation to sign since Yates and Lansing had already gone home. Afterward, Hamilton returned to New York and campaigned heavily for the document to be ratified by the state since the new constitution would not be nationally accepted without the approval of all thirteen states. Hamilton developed a small faction that verbally fought against Governor Clinton's supporters.

⊗

Two members of Hamilton's faction were John Jay and James Madison, who still had his doubts about Hamilton as a person but fervently supported the new Constitution. The trio wrote a series of intricate and thorough essays that defended the new iteration of the Constitution. These essays became known as the Federalist Papers and included 85 separate documents. Hamilton wrote the majority, having completed 51 in less than a year. Madison wrote 29 while Jay finished a measly 5, primarily because his areas of expertise were not as relevant as those of Hamilton and Madison. Hamilton remained in charge of the entire project and oversaw the publication of the essays while also enlisting new participants and divvying up the essays based on the different areas of experience of himself and the other two politicians.

⊗

So, Hamilton covered the executive and judicial branches of the federal government as well as matters related to taxation, the military, and certain parts of the Senate. Jay was in charge of foreign relations and interactions while Madison wrote about the checks and balances of the new federal government as well as the history of confederacies and republics. *The Independent Journal* published the papers throughout 1787. Hamilton signed the first one under the nom de plume Publius, and the other two men followed suit.

⊗

Eventually, New York voted to ratify the new iteration of the constitution 30 to 27 on July 26th, 1788. Hamilton would serve a second and final term in the Continental Congress under the original Articles of Confederation as the United States transitioned to a new government model.

۞

While he was arguing in favor of the new constitution, Hamilton was also fighting for the independence of Vermont. Back in 1764, King George settled a dispute between New York and New Hampshire over the region that would become known as Vermont. He ruled in favor of New York, and the state then refused to recognize property handed out to citizens by the government of New Hampshire in previous years. Over the next decade, strife broke out in the region and a faction attempted to establish a state government for a new place called Vermont. For eight years, the Continental Congress refused to recognize Vermont as a state since New York continued to claim the territory as its own.

۞

Around 1787, New York refused to abandon its claims to Vermont but had long given up on exerting control over the region. Hamilton argued that Vermont should be allowed to become a state because the territory of Kentucky was going to petition the new Congress for statehood. By Hamilton's logic, Kentucky would join the southern states and argue for their interests, so it would benefit the north to have another state sending representatives and senators to the federal government. He exchanged many letters with a lawyer representing the territory of Vermont, Nathaniel Chipman. Eventually, Hamilton's petitioning to the New York legislature paid off, and New York renounced its claims to Vermont in 1790.

❧ V ❧
A TITAN OF THE
TREASURY: REPORTS

"It's not tyranny we desire; it's a just, limited, federal government."

— ALEXANDER HAMILTON

❧

Following the Revolutionary War, George Washington was made the first president of the United States since he was the one figure the thirteen states could agree upon. He began to stock his Cabinet or the group of secretaries that would handle different aspects of the federal government. On September 11th, 1789, he made Hamilton the first-ever Secretary of the Treasury. Hamilton's term would be a difficult one since the structure of the government continued to be shaped and molded throughout Washington's five-year presidency. Historians tend to think that Hamilton considered his position to be similar to that of a British minister, and he thus strove to oversee his colleagues while remaining under the influence of Washington. Upon taking the position of Secretary of the Treasury, Hamilton immediately focused on his previous goals like strengthening the federal government. In particular, he wanted the government to be powerful through economic stability.

⚜

As the leader of a new treasury, Hamilton became responsible for defining the economic future of the nation. This would not be an easy feat. The states to the north and south possessed economies based on completely different factors and relied heavily on either industry or agrarianism to make money. Some members of the new government wanted the states to run independently, while others thought the country needed a powerful central government to keep everything in check. To examine all these factors and come up with a pleasing system required intense research, preparation, and a willingness to be shot down by critics. There also needed to be a simple way for Hamilton to communicate his ideas. These would be the reports. Hamilton wrote many of these documents during his five-year term. Each one laid out a new potential policy for the United States and included projections and materials that Congress could study in depth. Hamilton's writing commenced immediately upon his acceptance of the position of Secretary of the Treasury.

⚜

During one of the first meetings of the House of Representatives in September of 1789, the House asked Hamilton to write his first report. The subject was how the federal government could improve the public credit of the nation, and the deadline was January 1790. Hamilton had been considering this issue for almost a decade and sought out advice and suggestions from other influential thinkers of the time like James Madison and John Witherspoon. All three thought that extra taxes should be placed on the manufacture of alcohol as well as its importation into the new United States, but Madison expressed his concern that the securities from the debt of the government could be bought up by foreign powers – in other words, the United States would wind up owing more money to countries like France.

༄༅

Hamilton took such concerns seriously and wrote into his report that the securities from debts should be paid to their original owners and that the government should honor all its contracts even if it had difficulty paying. He viewed this as a matter of public and private morality. He further divided the country's debt into several groups: national, state, foreign, and domestic. The United States owed money to France, who had helped during the Revolutionary War, and already had a plan to pay the country back. The problem was that the new government had been paying soldiers and militia with promissory notes and IOUs. The soldiers, who needed to eat and feed their families, wound up selling the notes to speculators for pittances.

༄༅

In a move that demonstrated Hamilton's own privileged upbringing, he wrote that the government should pay the speculators and not the soldiers because the military men had shown such little faith in the government – never mind that they literally couldn't take care of themselves or their families. Hamilton also decided to combine state debts with the national debt and renamed it the federal debt to try to simplify the country's economy. This also diminished state power some, as the state debts came from trading with foreign nations as individual entities or from a failure to pay soldiers.

◈

When Hamilton submitted the report to the House of Representatives, it drew immediate consternation. Hamilton had once again drawn on British practices when developing his plan, and many detractors wanted to be as far away from the British as possible. Some argued that the plan also took power away from the representatives and gave it to the executive branch of government, which naturally angered those in the legislative branch. Others pointed out that many of Hamilton's friends were speculators who had purchased the debt of soldiers and would benefit from the new plan, thus calling Hamilton's character into question. Finally, representatives like Madison wanted the money from promissory notes to go to the original holders, claiming that the soldiers sold the notes out of necessity and desperation. His ideas were immediately defeated in a vote by the House.

◈

The next problem was that the states could not agree about whether the national government should assume state debts. Arguments lasted for over four months, during which the House requested that Hamilton explain just how this process was supposed to work. Overworked, Hamilton failed to deliver in time, and the House voted against the assumption.

A minor issue Hamilton did win, unrelated to his report, was convincing the House to temporarily move the capital of the United States to Philadelphia. The bill passed in July 1790.

۞

One month later, another measure suggested by Hamilton passed. To protect shipping to and from the United States, he suggested the creation of ten cutters, or ships designed to stop smuggling and piracy. Each cutter was stocked with well-armed men and cannonry to protect the interests of all states, from the tip of New England down to Georgia. Congress had no issue with the suggestion, and it went into effect on August 4th, 1790.

۞

The House of Representatives next asked Hamilton to craft a report on the potential for a national bank. Now, Hamilton had been thinking about a national bank for the United States for over a decade at this point. Ever since 1779, he had gathered and collected ideas from many different sources, drawing inspiration from famous philosopher and economist Adam Smith, the failures of the Bank of North America, the workings of the successful Bank of England, and his own work in helping establish the Bank of New York. He wrote to several confidantes and asked for their opinions but relied heavily on the inner mechanisms of his own mind and imagination to craft the idea he presented to the government.

۞

His report went as follows. Hamilton wanted Congress to charter a new National Bank with a capitalization of $10 million. The government would contribute 1/5 of that amount and, since it didn't have that kind of money, it would "***borrow***" the funds from the bank and repay the loan in ten installments. The other $8 million would be available to investors, and the bank's board of directors would consist of 25 independent members. Hamilton wanted these members to be private shareholders. He did not want the government to be involved in public debt. His vision was of a bank with a firm but elastic supply of funds which would contribute to economic development and the basic function of stable businesses. To get the tax revenue to start the bank, Hamilton once more suggested raising taxes and tariffs on alcohol.

❦

The Senate, upon reading the report, passed the bill immediately. As usual, the House of Representatives was full of objections. Representatives from the southern states believed Hamilton's bank only benefitted states to the north and completely ignored the agrarian economy prevalent in places like Virginia. Madison and Thomas Jefferson were fervent opponents, as were representatives who feared that any capital generated by the bank would stay in Philadelphia and never move to other states. Despite numerous protests and several angry and impassioned speeches, the bill to create the national bank passed with a magnificent vote of 39 to 20 on February 8th, 1791. Hamilton was thrilled and wrote of his success to multiple friends, believing the creation of the bank would contribute to a strong federal government – his ultimate goal.

❦

However, Hamilton still needed to get the bill past Washington, who hesitated when presented with it. Washington received advice from multiple parties like Hamilton, but also from people like Jefferson, who believed that the bank did not qualify as ***necessary and proper**" according to the Constitution. Hamilton retorted that a bank was necessary as a means of collecting taxes and creating one official account for the federal government. After much deliberation, Washington signed the bill into official law and the United States gained its national bank.

⚜

Although he celebrated his victory, Hamilton was not satisfied. Constantly working and ever the ambitious sort, he next set his eyes on the creation of a mint. Mints were and are the manufacturing centers of a nation's currency. Now that the United States was an official nation, it needed a legitimate currency approved of and backed by the federal government. Later in 1791, Hamilton presented his Report on the Establishment of a Mint to an awaiting House of Representatives. Once again, he drew inspiration from European models and economists, some of his friends, a few detractors like Jefferson, and the original resolutions from the Continental Congress in 1785 and 1786.

⚜

Hamilton drew inspiration from the current situation of the United States in the 1790s and suggested a plan which was realistic rather than idealistic. Since the most circulated coins at the time were Spanish, Hamilton wanted the minted U.S. dollar to weigh roughly the same amount as the standard Spanish peso. This made sense because currency at this time was minted on precious materials like silver and gold rather than being made of paper backed by a supply of metals held by the federal government. Hamilton additionally preferred silver to gold as the standard because the United States received a lot of silver from the West Indies. Another suggestion he included was the idea of minting coins with small values, such as a silver ten cent and single copper cent so poorer individuals would have experience handling money and could manage their expenses more accurately.

⚙

Surprisingly, Congress had fewer objections to Hamilton's currency ideas than they had about his national bank. In 1792, Congress accepted Hamilton's proposal and created the Coinage Act of 1792 as well as a new United States Mint.

⚙

The next report Hamilton submitted would be his Report on Manufactures on December 5th, 1791. Congress requested the document a year ago, but the subject was not an easy one. The federal government wanted to know whether it should become involved in the industrial work of the nation or if it should adopt a policy of noninterference. Hamilton fervently argued against noninterference and a sole focus on agrarianism, believing such a policy would be detrimental to trade with other nations. He also that manufacturing would be important when trying to carve out a place for the United States in the global industrial theater. Some of the suggestions he included for the federal government would be instituting high tariffs and duties on foreign manufactured goods that could also be produced in the United States, lowering the duties on raw materials sold within the country, and even encouraging immigration for people seeking employment in the United States.

Congress shelved his ideas for future consideration, and Hamilton pursued the development of American manufacturing on his own. In 1791, he and several colleagues from Philadelphia and New York formed the Society for the Establishment of Useful Manufactures. Contrary to its name, the Society was a private industrial corporation. In 1792, the directors met with Hamilton's father-in-law, Philip Schuyler, and scoped out a piece of property near the Passaic Falls in New Jersey for a new manufactory. Hamilton and his colleagues did manage to build their manufactory, but it failed quickly due to financial issues. Many shareholders refused to pay for their stocks, several members of the board went bankrupt, and the overseer of the program died in debtors' prison. Despite his best efforts, Hamilton could not keep his hopes of industrialization afloat.

❧ VI ❧

A TITAN OF THE TREASURY II: THE TWO-PARTY TANGO

"A well-adjusted person is one who makes the same mistake twice without getting nervous."

— ALEXANDER HAMILTON

❀

During his time as the Secretary of the Treasury, Hamilton found himself pitted against many of his contemporaries and participated in the shady dealings of politics. Upon his appointment in 1789, for example, Hamilton began to correspond with British agent Major George Beckwith, the same man who convinced well-known traitor Benedict Arnold to betray the Continental Army almost a decade earlier. In his letters, Hamilton revealed information discussed during secret Cabinet meetings to the British and notably misdirected President Washington about the nature of his correspondence. Why? To influence the direction the new United States would take when it came to foreign policy.

⚜

By all accounts, Hamilton viewed his work as absolutely essential. As stated earlier, he firmly believed that his work would shape the economy and policies of the United States. Due to his background in trade and finance, Hamilton focused heavily on realism when it came to commerce, trade, and foreign policy. He was challenged by notable Virginian agrarians like Thomas Jefferson and James Madison, who were more idealistic and wanted the nation to focus more on agriculture and the slave economy native to the southern states.

⚜

Starting in 1789, politicians like Hamilton and Jefferson began to separate themselves and form two rival parties, even though this behavior was exactly what the states had wanted to avoid. Hamilton's group named itself the Federalists after the ***Federalist Papers*** written previously. The Federalists wanted a strong national government protected by a national army and navy, as well as a government that was involved in the economy and foreign policy. Jefferson and Madison, meanwhile, headed a group known as the Democratic-Republican Party, shortened to the Republicans. Republicans wanted the opposite of the Federalists: strong state governments based in rural areas dedicated to agriculture, with state-sponsored militias and almost no navy to speak of.

⚜

Jefferson and Madison can be seen as Hamilton's two major enemies during his time as the Secretary of the Treasury. Both men denounced him frequently, claiming he was a monarchist who did not support the cause of republicanism. In particular, they believed he focused too much on cities, banking, business, and was far too friendly with Great Britain. In many regards, these claims were true – Hamilton was concerned about the future of the United States and felt that a good relationship with Great Britain was essential for protection and economic prosperity. He saw no potential in a purely agrarian society and likewise dismissed Madison and Jefferson as idealists with no practical life experience.

❧

At the beginning of his term, Hamilton started to assemble a nationwide coalition to support Washington's administration, including Hamilton's own financial programs and the president's decision to be neutral during the new war between Britain and France. He specifically attacked French agents like Citizen Genêt, who tried to convince American citizens directly to get involved in the war. Hamilton, like many other Federalists, wanted the new Americans to view themselves as national citizens of the United States, not of the countries their families might have migrated from. To bolster this, Hamilton additionally believed that a powerful national government dedicated to the principles of the Constitution was necessary.

❧

The Jeffersonian Republicans wanted to support France in its war against Britain since the French aided the United States during the American Revolution. They also wanted to shy away from policies that helped cities and did not want a national bank, which directly targeted Hamilton's policies. Both the Republicans and the Federalists began to build up political factions and developed their own newspapers to bolster their rhetoric and policies to the general public. These newspapers were anything but impartial; they were full of personal attacks, rumors, scandalous and invented claims, and deliberate exaggerations about the opposing political party. Hamilton created one in 1801, then called the New York Evening Post. It still exists, this time under the name of the New York Post.

৩৯৫৩

The fights and long-lasting rivalry between Alexander Hamilton and Thomas Jefferson truly shaped and defined American political history. Some historians even consider it to be the most important quarrel to ever happen in the country because the victor of their debates would have the power to shape the future of the entire nation. Their fighting was only enhanced by each man's desire to be Washington's most trusted advisor, as each man looked up to Washington and wanted to be the most influential person to the United States' most beloved figurehead.

৩৯৫৩

These party tensions heavily influenced Hamilton during his time as Secretary of the Treasury. Every time he submitted an economic report to Congress, it was guaranteed that the Republicans and Jefferson would have something to say. They constantly attempted to thwart Hamilton's plans and caused him no amount of stress during that period of his life. To make matters worse, in 1791, the Senate election in New York resulted in the election of partisan Republican Aaron Burr, who soundly defeated Hamilton's father-in-law. Hamilton personally blamed and took out the loss of the election on Burr, who he knew from previous engagements.

࿔

The next big issue in Hamilton's life was the creation of the Jay Treaty. When Great Britain and France went to war in 1793, Washington called for a meeting of his Cabinet and Hamilton attended. He and the others voted unanimously to adopt a position of neutrality because the United States did not have the resources necessary to fight a European war. Hamilton additionally voiced concerns about what might happen to the United States if Britain decided to retaliate by cutting off European trade to the states. The troublesome Citizen Genêt was sent home. The policy of neutrality lasted for about a year before new trade issues emerged in Congress in 1794. Hamilton and his Federalists found themselves fighting with the Republicans over trade with Britain. Hamilton wanted to increase trade with the powerful seafaring nation, while the Republicans proposed a trade war and declared Britain the ultimate threat to the republicanism of the United States.

࿔

Hamilton spoke at length with Washington about the issue. After some time, Washington decided to send Chief Justice John Jay to Great Britain to negotiate a future trade relationship. Before he left and while he was in Britain, Jay received the majority of his advice and instructions from Hamilton, who continued to push for better trade. The result was the Jay Treaty, which stated that relations between the two countries would include: most-favored-nation status for trading between the two countries, the evacuation of forts in the American northeast by the British, reparations paid by the British to the United States for its attacks on shipping, and repayment of old loan debts held by Americans to the British. The United States also received limited opportunities in the British West Indies and had to stop much of its trade with France.

⊗⊱⊗

This deal was great to Hamilton and the Federalists but enraged Republicans, who believed the United States was betraying France and the country's ideals for money. The Republicans denounced the treaty and tried to stop Congress from passing it, but Hamilton quickly mustered up the support needed. The Senate passed the Jay Treaty in 1795 with the bare minimum 2/3 majority needed to get it through the government. This treaty would become one of the United States and Hamilton's greatest victories, as it prevented another war with Britain and managed to bring the United States great economic prosperity.

⊗⊱⊗

The Jay Treaty's acceptance came after Hamilton finally decided to take a break, though. After spending so many years fighting for and trying to establish the American government and economic policies, he gave Washington two months' notice of his resignation on December 1st, 1794. This decision was heavily influenced by Eliza's miscarriage earlier in the year, which Hamilton had missed because he was occupied with political business.

In many ways, this halfway period in the 1790s could be seen as the beginning of Hamilton's downward spiral. While still a successful man, his ambition and tendency to overwork himself started to catch up with him. Combined with these pressures were his own personal flaws, such as his inability to withstand criticism without trying to drum up a response. Politically, he had done great work. But politics are always intertwined with personal attacks, affairs, and business, and this was exceptionally true of Hamilton.

❧ VII ❧

RESIGNATION, THE
REYNOLDS AFFAIR, AND
WOUNDS

"When the sword is once drawn, the passions of men observe no bounds of moderation."

— ALEXANDER HAMILTON

❧❧❧

Hamilton resumed his law practice in New York and stayed close to his family following his resignation. He continued to write and meet with Washington, whom he considered a close friend. He even drafted Washington's Farewell Address several times, and the two men compared ideas and what the Address would mean to a nation that was not ready to let go of the only non-partisan president the country would ever have. Since Washington resigned in 1796, a new presidential election occurred that same year.

Around this time, the United States had a different voting system which hadn't expected the presence of political parties. In fact, early drafts, documents, and even letters between the writers of the Constitution had indicated that the creators thought the idea of parties was disreputable and contradictory to the good of the nation. But Hamilton and Jefferson had created their Federalists and Republicans, and now they vied for power. Each person in Congress had two votes which they could use on two separate candidates. Whoever received the most votes would be president and whoever had the second most would be the vice president. The plan of the Federalists was to overwhelmingly vote for John Adams and then have a few people choose Thomas Pinckney as the vice president.

However, Hamilton didn't like John Adams and frequently spoke unfavorably about him to Washington. For his part, Adams also resented Hamilton and thought he was overambitious and improper. Hamilton conspired to have Pinckney receive more votes than Adams while still trying to keep Jefferson (the Republican choice) out of office. Unfortunately for him, the Federalists found out. The final results of the election ended with Adams as president but Jefferson as vice president. Adams' resentment and hatred of Hamilton grew.

This would not be the only blunder or mistake in Hamilton's grand designs and intrigue. The next year, 1797, Hamilton became embroiled in the first major sex scandal in the history of the United States, when it was revealed that he had become involved with a woman eleven years younger than him in 1791. The affair was with a woman named Maria Reynolds, who was married but claimed her husband abandoned her. She solicited monetary aid from Hamilton but then quickly developed a sexual relationship. Her husband, James, soon found out and requested Hamilton pay him $1000 in exchange for his silence about the matter.

❦

Hamilton paid but then resumed his visits to Maria. James continued to solicit money from him until Hamilton ended the affair a year later. For five years, the incident remained a secret from everyone, including Eliza. However, James Reynolds and his friend Jacob Clingman were arrested in November 1792 under charges of counterfeiting money and illegal speculation. When Clingman made bail, he immediately went to politician James Monroe and explained that the imprisoned Reynolds had information about Hamilton that could incriminate the other man. Monroe spoke of the issue with several other congressmen. The trio seemed to believe that Hamilton was involved in some form of speculation and illegal money handling. In December, they confronted Hamilton.

❦

Hamilton revealed the affair, ending the rumors about illegal speculation or mismanagement of the national treasure. As evidence, he showed the other congressmen the letters he exchanged with Maria and James Reynolds and explained that the payments made were blackmail. Monroe and the other congressmen were to keep the documents a secret from everyone, and they did for the next five years.

❧

Unfortunately for Hamilton's desired secrecy, a journalist by the name of James Callender published a document called "*A History of the United States for the Year 1796*." Within its pages were accusations that the imprisoned Reynolds had been an agent of Hamilton's that misused treasury funds. Hamilton, who could not handle criticism or rumors well, decided the best course of action that summer of 1797 was to publish a 100-page booklet that explicitly described and discussed his affair with Maria Reynolds.

❧

The reaction was immediate. Hamilton became the laughing-stock of the Republican party, who believed his actions were immoral and imprudent – the affair and the decision to publish such a long document about it. Many of Hamilton's friends and colleagues were disgusted with his behavior and some, like Monroe, never forgave his impropriety. Surprisingly, many others remained unaffected, including Washington. As for his family, Eliza packed up and moved away from her husband, choosing to live apart from him for at least a year. She eventually forgave him and returned to live with him, but he did not regain her trust for some time. As for Hamilton's children, the younger did not quite understand the situation, but the older were disappointed, especially Hamilton's oldest son.

❧

Hamilton remained out of the spotlight for a few months following the revelation of the affair and stayed focus on his law practice. He did not return to any major political actions until he was made a major general of the United States' army by President Adams. Why? The United States was facing a potential French invasion during an incident called the Quasi-War of 1798-1800.

❦

The Quasi-War began following the infamous French Revolution when the monarchy fell, and several republics developed in France in rapid succession. The United States refused to keep paying off the debt it owed France from its assistance during the American Revolution, claiming the money was owed to an old regime. This angered the new French government, and it sent its navy to attack American ships.

❦

Hamilton became the inspector general of the army until the war's end. Since Washington did not want to leave his home at Mount Vernon unless actual fighting broke out, Hamilton became the de facto leader of the military, which displeased Adams. Hamilton frequently fought with Adams, much as he fought with other politicians because he believed he had better ideas about the direction the country needed to take. If a full war broke out with France, Hamilton wanted to march his troops down to the colonies of France's ally, Spain, and take that territory. He was additionally prepared to quash any resistance in the southern United States if that section of the country did not agree with his and Adams' decisions. To fund the army, Hamilton harassed the new Secretary of the Treasury, a man named Wolcott.

Hamilton never received his chance to march down to the Spanish colonies. Adams, who did not want a full-scale war with France, opened negotiations with the other nation in 1800. France sued for peace, and the Quasi-War came to an end. Hamilton's army was disbanded, much to his annoyance. Adams, meanwhile, fired several of his cabinet members, believing they were far more loyal to Hamilton than to him. Hamilton went back to his law practice with his hopes of more military glory quashed and his friends in the Cabinet thrown out.

Hamilton's animosity with Adams came to the forefront later that year, when the Federalists sought to reelect Adams as president during the 1800 presidential election. This time, the two Federalists up for election were John Adams and a man named Charles Pinckney, who was the elder brother of Thomas, the man who ran for vice president during the 1796 election. Hamilton once again attempted to convince more Federalists to cast their votes for Pinckney than Adams and wrote to congressmen from South Carolina with the same idea. He went so far as to create a pamphlet entitled "***Letter from Alexander Hamilton, Concerning the Public Conduct and Character of John Adams, Esq. President of the United States.***" The entire pamphlet was extremely critical but did reluctantly endorse Adams at the end. He mailed it to two hundred other Federalists, but a copy came into the position of the Republican party. They published it, damaging Hamilton's reputation among the Federalists.

The Federalists became divided, and the Republican nominees won instead. Thomas Jefferson and Aaron Burr received the same number of votes in the Electoral College, and Hamilton became the deciding vote over who would become president. He chose Jefferson, despite the two men's animosity, believing him to be less of a threat than Burr. However, soon Jefferson became unwilling to support Burr as the vice president and made it clear that he would not be chosen as Jefferson's partner in the 1804 election.

❧

Hamilton's joy from his political victory was short-lived. In 1801, his oldest son met with an opponent to duel over a matter of honor. Philip, the same son who had been disappointed with his father years ago, was shot and killed at the age of 21. Hamilton and Eliza mourned for months, even as another child was born to the couple shortly after Philip's death. Once again, Hamilton withdrew from political life for a little while but rapidly returned. He was like a machine, constantly needing to be in motion.

❧

Burr, desperate for some political office, instead ran for governor of New York in the 1804 election. Hamilton heavily worked against him, writing letters to many individuals throughout the state to destroy Burr's political base. When some of these documents came to light, Burr suspected his honor had been attacked and demanded an apology from Hamilton, preferably in a letter. Hamilton responded with a letter claiming that he knew of no such instance where he insulted Burr. Although the two men sought several forms of reconciliation, neither was willing to admit they were wrong.

Eventually, they decided to end the issue the gentlemanly way: a duel.

❧

Hamilton valued his honor and had, in fact, been part of seven previous matters of honor, most of which did not result in duels. Before the duel took place, he wrote out a letter to his family, explaining his decision to go through with the duel but fully intending to throw his shot – in other words, deliberately miss. Hamilton valued his role as a father, husband, and lawyer and did not want to compromise his family's welfare. However, he thought the duel was necessary because he had insulted Burr and it was the moral thing to do. He had no intention of killing Burr, primarily because he wished to be involved in future political endeavors and it would look back if he murdered his opponent.

❧

The duel took place on July 11th, 1804 along the west bank of the Hudson River. Sadly, the duel took place near the place where Hamilton's oldest son, Philip, died three years previously. Hamilton and Burr both fired: Hamilton's shot struck a tree above Burr's head, while Burr directly shot Hamilton in the lower abdomen. Several of his ribs fractured, and the bullet ricocheted internally, causing severe damage to several organs. Eventually, the bullet became lodged in Hamilton's spine, paralyzing him. No one knew who fired first. Historians speculate that Burr fully intended to hit and kill Hamilton, especially since he wore his glasses and took his time to aim the shot.

❧

Friends carried the injured and dying Hamilton to the nearby Greenwich Village. He laid in the home of his friend, William Bayard Jr. Eliza and their children appeared shortly after hearing the news to say their goodbyes. Accounts indicate that Eliza, who was beside herself, chastised Hamilton for his decision in her grief. More friends arrived to also say farewell to Hamilton throughout the day and well into the evening. After more than twenty-four hours of suffering, Hamilton died the next day at 2:00 pm on July 12th, 1804. He was buried shortly afterward in the Trinity Churchyard Cemetery.

❧ VIII ☙
A FLAWED MAN
THROUGH AND
THROUGH

"Learn to think continentally."

— ALEXANDER HAMILTON

❧❧❧

Alexander Hamilton left behind an impressive legacy, in no small part due to his success in defining the economic and political systems of the United States. This legacy was especially important to Hamilton's family. His wife, Eliza, lived an additional forty years following Hamilton's death and strove to preserve the memory of her husband by publishing many of his papers and documents. Hamilton's *Federalist Papers* continue to be the basis for Constitutional interpretation and court decisions throughout the nation, and his creation of a national bank and decision to support a strong federal power over states' power helped lay the groundwork for what could be considered a national issue over a state issue. However, his reputation wasn't always so golden.

☙❧

Up until the 20th century, Hamilton was seen as dangerously aristocratic and downright conservative, someone who would strengthen the federal government to the point of tyranny. He was a threat and the embodiment of everything wrong with the original British system of government which had plagued the thirteen colonies that formed the United States. It wasn't until the Progressive era that Hamilton gained the support of historians and politicians like Theodore Roosevelt, who saw the bonuses and benefits to be obtained from a powerful centralized government. Nowadays, it's not uncommon for historians and professors to show Hamilton as an energetic and visionary architect of the contemporary capitalist United States. His archenemy Jefferson, meanwhile, is seen as a naïve, hypocritical dreamer in numerous academic circles.

☙❧

Perhaps because of his creation of a national bank, designers depicted Hamilton on more currency notes than any other figure in history. As of 2018, he has appeared at different times on the $2, $5, $10, $20, $50, and $1,000 bills. In modern times, he is on the $10 bill, where he has remained since 1928. As a fun historical note, the U.S. Treasury planned to remove him from the $10 bill in 2015 and replace his image with that of Harriet Tubman, but the unprecedented success of ***Hamilton: An American Musical*** meant he kept his place. Hamilton also appeared on a few commemorative stamps, but none more recent than 1957.

❧

Multiple statues and memorials exist to honor Hamilton, both in the United States and the former British West Indies. People can find statues in Central Park, at the U.S. Treasury in Washington D.C., in Lincoln Park, and at the Paterson Great Falls National Historical Park near Hamilton's failed business venture. His historic home was restored to its original appearance in 2011 and is now the Hamilton Grange National Memorial in St. Nicholas Park. Although his childhood home in Charlestown on the island of Nevis was destroyed long ago, the government built a new center called Hamilton House that is currently the site of the Alexander Hamilton Museum. The second floor is the meeting place for the Nevis Island Assembly.

❧

Interpretations of Alexander Hamilton's character vary. Although he appeared in a few television dramas and movies during the 20th century and even had a musical in 1917, he wasn't a well-known figure outside of historical circles. Many might have heard the name, but few could actually say who he was and what he did. Now, in the contemporary world with the success of a new musical, it's not uncommon for people to make their judgments about Hamilton's character based on the show and not the actual man. So, what were the real Alexander Hamilton's strengths and weaknesses?

❧

Individuals can certainly draw inspiration from Hamilton's persistence, tenacity, ambition, and discipline. Although he did begin with a relatively privileged background in the 18th century – his father and mother both had noble ancestry, he received an education, he was white and an English citizen – he still needed to work to earn his position. He overcame his illegitimate heritage and studied rigorously while in the British colonies to gain a better understanding of government and economics. He joined the American Revolution even though most people thought it would fail and he would be punished with quartering and death. His ambition drove him to marry a wealthy woman, get in good with the right people, and eventually become a Founding Father. Such a fate would not have been possible if he had kept his head down and accepted his life in Nevis.

◈

With such a background and ambition though, it should come as no surprise that Hamilton's greatest flaw was his pride. He knew that his accomplishments were unusual and unprecedented. He strove to defend his reputation at all costs and was willing to hurt those around him if it meant he could hold his head high and claim to be serving the good of the country – for example, the Reynolds Affair. More importantly, his pride and arrogance would lead to his death through his duel with Aaron Burr. While being a proud man, he was additionally plagued by feelings of worthlessness and inadequacy, no doubt fueled by his illegitimate background and difficulties relating to the other nobles who formed the Constitutional Congress and early American government.

◈

These volumes offer a fuller picture of the life of Alexander Hamilton and the various factors that combined to make the life of such a driven, intriguing man.

❧ IX ❧
FURTHER READING

❦

People who would like to learn more about Alexander Hamilton can check out other biographies, such as:

- Ron Chernow's *Alexander Hamilton*
- Charles A. Conant's *Alexander Hamilton*
- Michael W. Simmons' *Alexander Hamilton: First Architect of the American Government*

YOUR FREE EBOOK!

As a way of saying thank you for reading our book, we're offering you a free copy of the below eBook.

Happy Reading!

Made in the USA
Middletown, DE
11 December 2020